THE
WHITE LIGHT
of GRACE

ALSO BY LILLIE LEONARDI

*In the Shadow of a Badge: A Memoir
about Flight 93, a Field of Angels
and My Spiritual Homecoming*

Available at your local bookstore,
or may be ordered by visiting:

Hay House UK: www.hayhouse.co.uk
Hay House USA: www.hayhouse.com®
Hay House Australia: www.hayhouse.com.au
Hay House India: www.hayhouse.co.in

THE
WHITE LIGHT
of GRACE

reflections on the life of a
spiritual intuitive

LILLIE LEONARDI

HAY HOUSE

Carlsbad, California • New York City • London • Sydney
Johannesburg • Vancouver • Hong Kong • New Delhi

First published and distributed in the United Kingdom by:
Hay House UK Ltd, Astley House, 33 Notting Hill Gate, London W11 3JQ
Tel: +44 (0)20 3675 2450; Fax: +44 (0)20 3675 2451; www.hayhouse.co.uk

Published and distributed in the United States of America by:
Hay House Inc., PO Box 5100, Carlsbad, CA 92018-5100
Tel: (1) 760 431 7695 or (800) 654 5126
Fax: (1) 760 431 6948 or (800) 650 5115; www.hayhouse.com

Published and distributed in Australia by:
Hay House Australia Ltd, 18/36 Ralph St, Alexandria NSW 2015
Tel: (61) 2 9669 4299; Fax: (61) 2 9669 4144; www.hayhouse.com.au

Published and distributed in the Republic of South Africa by:
Hay House SA (Pty) Ltd, PO Box 990, Witkoppen 2068
info@hayhouse.co.za; www.hayhouse.co.za

Published and distributed in India by:
Hay House Publishers India, Muskaan Complex, Plot No.3, B-2,
Vasant Kunj, New Delhi 110 070
Tel: (91) 11 4176 1620; Fax: (91) 11 4176 1630; www.hayhouse.co.in

Distributed in Canada by:
Raincoast Books, 2440 Viking Way, Richmond, B.C. V6V 1N2
Tel: (1) 604 448 7100; Fax: (1) 604 270 7161; www.raincoast.com

Text © Lillie Leonardi, 2016

Cover design: Karla Baker • Interior design: Pamela Homan

The moral rights of the author have been asserted.

A catalogue record for this book is available from the British Library.

ISBN: 978-1-78180-176-5

Printed and bound in Great Britain by TJ International, Padstow, Cornwall.

ACKNOWLEDGMENTS

To my daughter, for helping me become a better human being.

To my beloved grandchildren,
for teaching your grandmother about love.

To my parents, thank you for this wonderful life.

To my siblings, for sharing in the
positive and negative aspects of life.

To Dr. Deborah Conway, June Esser, Dr. Pamela Moalli,
Dr. Jonathan Pallone, Dr. Darryl Reed, Dr. Maryellen Schroeder,
and Andrea Shafran, the dedicated medical professionals
who aided me on my journey to heal.

To Cynthia Cannell, for reminding me to believe in myself.

To Sally Mason, for helping to fine-tune this book.

To Selina Blinn, Beth Caldwell, Jean Haller, and
Karen Stone, for helping to network my works.

To Beth Mellor, for providing a quiet environment to write.

To Judy and Phil Sobo, for offering a safe harbor to pen pages.

To Buck and Jo Ann Courter, Penny Harrington, Cally Jamis
Vennare, Mirna Solorzano, Teresa Stitt, Michele Traficante, and
Connie Valenti, for your fellowship.

To Samantha Coury, for your
invaluable assistance and patience.

To Sam Coury, for your unending
guidance in all things great and small.

And

To all of my brothers and sisters in law
enforcement; it was an honor to serve with you.

May God send the Archangel Michael to keep watch
over one and all as you answer your call to service.

Blessings . . .

CONTENTS

PREFACE

I often feel as if I have lived two separate lives. One in the physical, where I learned how to live in my humanity, and the other in the metaphysical, where I lived in the "afterward" of all that I had learned, thus allowing for the evolution of my spirit. Enclosed in the chapters of this book are the stories of my life—a life I viewed and watched play out with great passion and sentiment. The chapters are distinctive in their perspective of my early years of life, when it seemed that I saw life in a black-and-white cascade of events. Based on my strict Catholic upbringing, there was a right way and a wrong way to conduct myself. As I matured and grew into the woman I am today, I saw life's events were not all black and white, but that they had many gray areas of choice mixed with twists of fate, a little bit of luck, and some grace as well. My life's work also had an added touch of blue, signifying my years serving as a law enforcement professional, which gave a new dimension to my observations of life and its purpose.

This book is also a love story of sorts. It is not the conventional type that you may be familiar with reading. It is, however, my rendition of all of my "affairs of the heart" that have touched my life and etched themselves into my memory. These chapters provide a look at the inner sanctum of all of the various loves in my life. Each is individually defined, respected, and valued for the lessons I learned about myself and others. Despite the good, the bad, or the ugly of the relationships, each of these persons is to be credited with helping me to become a better person and for enriching my life. They are responsible for my ability to see that we must live with the love we have been given—because love is a blessing in any form. We must cherish each moment with those we love, for time passes by all too quickly. And we must learn to hold all of the memories of loved ones close to our hearts.

Additionally, the stories in this book provide insight and testimony into my spiritual life. Since early childhood, I have heard the whispers of angels and, on occasion, witnessed manifestations in the darkness of the night. While I was huddling in my bed, a spirit would illuminate the shadows, enshrouded by the loveliest cobalt blue aura, and ease away my fears. When I asked the celestial visitor his name, I heard the word "Michael" softly whispered in my ear.

In my juvenescence, I truly believed the apparition to be that of an angelic being, the Archangel Michael. During that time in my life, my innocent mind and open heart did indeed prevail. As I grew into my adolescent years, the angel would still speak to me, but I began to have my doubts. Over time, I learned to trust in the wisdom of the angel's words, for in them came messages of truth not only about me, but about others as well. Archangel Michael became my devoted friend, trusted protector, and guide. On all too many occasions, I have heard his voice whispering in my ear some form of guidance or words of wisdom that aided me in a given situation. Archangel Michael was—and continues to be—a guiding beacon of light in my spiritual enlightenment. Through him, I have come to know and better understand God. My faith in the Creator has increased, as has my relationship with the Divine.

As I share these chapters of my life, memories slip by my mind's eye, both joyful and sad in nature. Interlaced with these stories of grace and ambivalence are those that threatened my safe passage through a maze of intermittent creativity and harsh reality. These stories provide a perspective on complexities that have taken me years to comprehend.

When reading through the passages, you may note that the book is not always written in a chronological style, but rather, in a method that links the various stages of my life and the pivotal points of transition that allowed me to evolve. It is my hope that this book of personal reflection may open your mind to contemplating how one life can affect the balance of all. It is now clear to me that age, gender, race, and religion have little bearing on the spirit that lives within each of us—our spirit is the foundation that distinguishes us as individuals and also links us to each other. In life, we may each perceive ourselves as singular in design, but we are all one organism, all interwoven and set to work in unity and responsible one for the other.

In scribing these pages, I finally learned to let go. To release the past mistakes, regrets, shame, and hurts that had accumulated over a lifetime. With each chapter written, I relived the moments that had negatively impacted me for all too long. As the pen glided across the lines of the paper, the words flowed and I felt the pent-up emotions drift away. I laughed. I cried. I procrastinated. I bellowed in anger. I recalled with vivid fervor the impressions that these events left embedded over time. As my mind released the anguish, I felt my heart reawaken. I allowed myself to feel the bounty of my heart and soul. And on one glorious morning, I fell to my knees in praise, raised my arms toward Heaven, and rejoiced in the House of Elohim.

CHAPTER 1

THE ORIGINS
OF GRACE

Every morning I open the window blinds of my home, bend on one knee, bow my head, and greet the Blessed Mother by saying, "Good morning, my beloved mother and friend." As I look across the grassy knoll of my back-yard, I gaze at a lovely statue of Mary, the Queen of Angels. Next to the statue is a figurine of an angel that was placed there to guard Mary.

Since the fall of 2001, this effigy of Mother Mary has stood there, upon the stones of a small grotto. It was erected to honor Her and to give sanctuary to myself and others in a time of need. Each morning I bid Mary a good day, and every night a restful slumber. I ask Her to surround me with Her blue robe of protection and Her white light of grace. In invoking Mary, I instantly feel the warmth of Her light encompass my entire being, and I feel enshrouded by Her comforting love.

Since my earliest recollections, I have been graced by the white light from Heaven above. Although for many years I did not understand what a blessed life I have lived, I have come to comprehend it now. At the age of 16, I first began my relationship with Mary. Our alliance was forged after my mother gifted me with a small prayer book to honor Our Lady of Perpetual Help. Over the years, this strong bond has aided me in better understanding my spiritual path and purpose. Through it, I learned to accept that life has many mysteries that do not always allow for an explanation or even make sense. Sometimes, there seem to be no clear reasons for what transpires. However, I now believe that the answers to all questions are ever present—that is, if we are willing to listen to the inner wisdom of our souls.

This amazing bond with Mother Mary was not, however, the initial spiritual connection I felt with the heavenly realm. As a child, I felt the magnificent presence of the Archangel Michael, and often confided this belief in others. When first I told my parents about the encounters, my mother said they were just a part of my "overactive imagination." She would often berate me and caution me not to share the details of the angelic encounters with others. In her own way, Mom was trying to protect me, but I felt she had somehow betrayed me as well. For in my mind, I knew what I professed about the Archangel to be true. When Archangel Michael would appear in the corner of my bedroom, I would instantly feel the warmth of his being. In turn, I would feel an inner connection to him and the illumination of my soul.

As I moved through my childhood years, Archangel Michael appeared many times. On those occasions, I would jump out of bed and wake my parents to inform them that the angel, who I referred to as the "Blue Man with wings," had visited. In order to appease me, Dad would often return to my room with me. Once there, he would conduct a ritual of looking under the bed and inside the closet—all the while explaining that there was no blue man. Although Dad could not see what I saw, I knew that Archangel Michael was present.

As time passed, I received many reprimands about my declarations referencing Archangel Michael and his appearances. Eventually, I stopped sharing my experiences with others. Instead, I would retreat to the isolation of my room and contemplate all that had occurred. Yet, despite my parents' continued rejections of my belief in the angelic encounters, I was convinced the Archangel Michael was real. My bedroom became a sanctuary where I could read books and jot down my thoughts. Before too long, I began to take comfort in solitude over family and friends. In those moments, I felt even more connected to the higher power of God. It seemed as if I had an energy that flowed to me, through me, and permeated every aspect of my being. And although my youthful mind was not able to fully comprehend angelic channeling, I was astute enough to recognize that something amazing was transpiring.

So in the midst of a traditional lifestyle came the growing feeling that I was different from my siblings. Although I enjoyed moments of childhood glee, I found little pleasure in the things that made most children happy. I seemed to relish my time alone and the beauty of nature. The simple things in life brought such pleasure to me. Whenever possible, I would retreat to my bedroom so that I could read, write, and dream of the angels. Over time, I would come to realize that the angels and their whispers held the key to my intuitive gifts. And I soon learned that the magic that was within me was also a part of certain other members of my family.

As a young woman, I had the pleasure of spending time with my grandmother Situ. *Situ* is the Arabic word for grandmother. In my eyes, Situ was the wisdom keeper of our family. Although she had a limited formal education, my grandmother was brilliant about topics related to human nature and matters of the heart. She was small in stature, but her heart was large—as was the energy emitted from her person. Her smile was warm and her embrace even warmer. And when I sat next to her, I felt a connection that seemed to link our spirits as one. Like many family elders, Situ shared stories about our ancestors. On one soft summer's evening as we sat on the back porch of her home, she shared with me the folklore that had been passed down from *her* elders. She explained how our family that dwelled in the Middle East had been members of the early Christian movement. According to the legend, our family could be traced back unto the time that Jesus walked the earth.

In 1913, she and my grandfather emigrated from Lebanon. Like other immigrants during that time period, they arrived at Ellis Island. There, among the thousands of other travelers, they were led toward a passageway that represented a new life. Our family name was originally spelled Khouri, which means "priest" in Arabic. It is a surname unique to Arab Christians and was often given as a last name to a new priest. It is common practice for a family to keep the surname even after the cleric has passed. According to my grandmother, these priests were also considered to be "bearers of light." The generations that followed after these early Christians chose to practice the Maronite Catholic religion, and until the time of my father's death, it was the doctrine of choice.

When I questioned Situ's accounting, she asked me not to doubt her portrayal of the family legacy. She urged me to believe, to have faith, and, when it was time to do so, to pass the birthright on to the next generation. Over time, I have come to realize that this white light of grace has been a blessing on my family. This legacy is the reason why certain of my family members are open to their intuitive gifts. And according to my grandmother, these gifts often skip generations. In contemplating her statement, I can see that this lineage has indeed been a part of the gift. That is, as it relates to the present generations. Although I see traces in some, I have not observed the same level of ability in each. Some were raised to fear it. Some have chosen to ignore it. Others considered it to be against their religious beliefs. And then there are those like myself, who have discovered what an amazing gift it truly is.

If indeed the stories of the long-ago ancestors are factual, the light that was born in the early days of our heritage still illuminates the present generations. My dad often expressed his thoughts about the subject in a different manner. "Prayer is not only recited for the benefit of the present generation," he told me. "It is done to pray for those who have passed, for those who live today, and for those who will be born in the future. Prayer is a good deed passed on for three generations." And so, the continuous prayers of my ancestors have graced each generation that followed.

Grace is defined as the free and unmerited favor of God and the bestowal of His blessings. In contemplating this definition, I find myself better able to comprehend the miracles that have occurred throughout my lifetime.

Whenever a problematic situation arose, I looked inward to the strength of my spirit and upward for the divine intervention of God. In doing so, I was able to work through difficult situations that would have otherwise led my life astray. Equally, my beliefs and faith in the higher power of God allowed for me to move forward after each and every trial and tribulation tested my faith.

Throughout these many years, I did spend a fair part of my life pushing away the sensations and connections that have since come to define me. But on September 11, 2001, my life was dramatically altered. While serving with the Federal Bureau of Investigation on 9/11 at the Flight 93 crash site in Shanksville, Pennsylvania, I witnessed a legion of angels. My life instantaneously became multidimensional and shattered in all that was familiar. In trying to comprehend my vision on that fateful day, I have struggled with the burden of having such a profound experience. This required me to dig deep within, to the inner recesses of my heart and soul. Once there, my present life collided with the past, and the portals to my memories filled with all too many recollections. Through my introspective journey, I grew to believe that we all carry a gift within us. Sometimes, our ability to access it is lost to us due to everyday situations and stressors in life. But sometimes, the tragedies in our lives awaken these abilities to feel, hear, and see the presence of God and sense His universal power.

I believe that we are all guided and protected by God's winged messengers, the angels. If we are open to them, we have the ability to communicate with these celestial beings. Some of my earliest memories are of feeling their touches and hearing their whispers. They keep watch over us and over those beings who have left this earthly domain.

Like many, my life's story is complex and filled with joys and sorrows. But I have learned that it takes but a moment in time to discover one's purpose. Purpose implies a spiritual intention, a goal that helps define why an individual chose to travel to this earthly plane. As the chapters of this book unfold, so will the segments of my personal story about falling from grace to understanding that I never really fell—I merely strayed. It took almost a lifetime for me to acknowledge the gifts I have been given, to fully trust and believe that the white light of grace comes in many forms. This journey of reconciliation has now come full circle, and I am so grateful for the grace bestowed on not only me, but also on my family.

I now fully embrace that conversation of so long ago with Situ. There, on her back porch with the soft scents of summer in the air, she shared stories of our family's legacy. And there, surrounded by her lovely rose garden, my soul began to blossom and an awakening of spiritual interconnection took root.

CHAPTER 2

FIRST HOLY COMMUNION

"For by Him were all things created, that are in heaven, and that are in earth, visible and invisible, whether they be thrones, or dominions, or principalities, or powers: all things were created by Him, and for Him."

~ COLOSSIANS 1:16

Throughout my life, countless individuals have asked me what it was like to grow up in a home overrun with nine siblings. The best way to describe the household is "functionally dysfunctional." In my reflection on my upbringing, there are many wonderful memories of childhood interlaced with heartache and drama, too. These impressions remain embedded in my mind and tightly bound to the individuals whom I fondly call family.

My parents were married in the Catholic Church. Like many other devout Catholic couples, they immediately began procreating. Over the course of eleven years, ten children were born. The family was a perfect complement of five boys and five girls. Although our family bore a resemblance to many large Catholic families of the 1950s, it also comprised a character all its own. It was our version of *All in the Family* and we wore the title well. Our living accommodations also resembled that of an ancestral tribe. My maternal grandparents lived in an apartment adjoining the house. My paternal grandmother lived across the street, and an aunt and her five children lived next door.

Like so many other men of his era, Dad had served in the military during World War II. Post serving in the Army Air Corps, Dad returned home and attended college. He received a degree and became an educator and businessman as well. After bearing ten children, Mom returned to college and obtained several degrees. She became a professor and taught both music and theater on a college campus.

From my parents, I acquired knowledge about the world and the role I would eventually play in it. They helped define the importance of finding purpose and serving mankind and the greater good. They instilled in me core values about God, religion, family, education, and integrity. Based on the moral compass that my parents fostered, I grew to better understand the concepts of honoring God and providing service. Through their teachings, my soul began its journey, a pilgrimage that allowed my heart to open, my mind to question, and my spirit to seek answers.

As a result of my parents' tutelage my belief in God was forged, as was my faith in His winged messengers. I no longer practice religion in the same manner that I was instructed to as a young girl in Catholic school, but I do worship and pray with deep conviction. Through my parents' practice of Catholicism, I was afforded an opportunity to enrich my soul. This unearthed a path that led to my spiritual enlightenment.

My first recollection of sensing the presence of my guardian angel was during the church ceremony for my first Holy Communion. I remember the service as if it were yesterday. The date was May 11, 1963, and it also happened to be my seventh birthday. I was wearing a lovely white dress; a veil; and matching shoes, gloves, and purse. Inside my tiny purse decorated with yellow flowers rested my new prayer book, a rosary, and a handkerchief—all white. I remember making a fuss with my mother because I hated wearing dresses. A typical seven-year-old tomboy, I would much rather be wearing shorts and a T-shirt, playing football and climbing trees. But as usual, Mom won the argument.

When we arrived at the church, I saw all of my classmates lined up, readying to march up the aisle. The clergy members were preparing for the procession as well. Attired in their ceremonial garb, they looked both regal and intimidating. All too soon, it seemed, the music began to play. The familiar notes of the organ blasted the opening song. The altar boys were first in line to move forward into the church, and they were followed by the clergy. Then came the communicants' turn. I recall marching up the aisle and feeling very awkward. I walked past my family, sitting in the same exact pew that we sat in during weekly Sunday worship. I saw my dad and mom smiling proudly as I passed them by. I tried my best not to focus on them, but rather on those who were leading the procession. The mass and the service began, and soon it was time to receive my first Holy Communion. As I exited the pew, I felt exceptionally anxious about remembering what I was supposed to do once I got to the altar.

When I approached the bishop and he extended his hand toward me, I opened my mouth to receive the host. I heard my shaky voice utter the word "amen." I then turned to march across the front of the altar and down the side aisle. At that moment, my mind became confused and I hesitated. All of a sudden, I heard a male voice whisper, "Turn this way."

With the words softly echoing in my ear, my entire being became very warm. Then it felt as if an invisible hand was placed upon my shoulder gently guiding me in the appropriate direction. With that touch, my whole body became electrified with a wonderful energy. At that point in my life, I was unaware that this was the magic of an angel's touch. Yet despite my childhood naïveté, I was somehow astute enough to truly comprehend that I had experienced divine intervention.

Following the church service, my family and friends gathered at my parents' home to celebrate both my communion and birthday. As we arrived at the house, my dad gave me a hug and complimented me on my march. He remarked that he was very impressed by how I had remembered all the cues and maintained my posture, much like a soldier. It was then that I told him about what I had heard and felt in the church.

Dad laughed and said, "It must have been your guardian angel."

I smiled back at him and meekly replied, "It was."

For most of my life, I have shared a special relationship with the Archangel Michael. During both good and bad times, I have felt his presence and invoked his protection. Over these many years, he has helped me in innumerable ways. In the early stages of our alliance, I did not comprehend the magnitude of his guidance in all things great and small. However, as I grew toward a more spiritual existence, I became better able to understand the synchronicity and connection I had with this beloved, angelic being. As I reminisce now about the many days in my life in which I have witnessed the presence of an angel, I marvel at all the blessings I have received. In countless moments when I was most in need, my prayers were always answered. And on that day of my first Holy Communion, I was first guided by the gentle coddling of a warm hand and a soft, dulcet voice. That voice and touch have remained with me for many years.

It now seems ironic that on the day I first sensed the touch of the Archangel was almost the exact moment when I received the host. It is my belief that these two events are symbolic of the merging of the heart and the soul. Perhaps it was in that precise moment that I came to understand the oneness of my humanity and my spirituality, and accepted that guardian angels are ever vigilant. They serve to guide, protect, heal, and help us manifest our dreams.

CHAPTER 3

A CHILD
WITHIN A CHILD

Like most marriages, mine began with feelings of both hope and trepidation. Even though the situation was not ideal—we were just teenagers, expecting an unplanned child—our union was nonetheless a result of two hearts merging as one. As we settled into our marriage, however, that hope began to fade. The meaning behind the words "I do" became a distant memory. As time progressed, life with my husband became a continuous series of battles borne of irreconcilable differences. Time became our enemy, and the love we had felt on our wedding day dissipated a little more with each disagreement. Our marriage and our home quickly became a battleground filled with echoes of anger.

In the months following the wedding, I had tried very hard to acclimate to my new surroundings. For the first time in my life, I had left the security of my parents' home. I felt lost and alone in a strange new milieu. The tension felt over the marriage was still viewed as a negative factor in all our lives. All the turmoil and transition made me miss all that had been familiar to me even more—including the heartfelt connection to my angelic guide, which seemed to diminish as my fear and sadness increased.

After our short honeymoon, my husband and I moved in with his parents and two younger siblings. Although his family's home was quite lavish and stylish, it seemed to lack any meaningful sense of warmth. From the moment I entered the home, it was obvious that my new mother-in-law ruled the roost. If and when she became upset with me, I knew my husband would be helpless to defend me.

My husband came from a family that was familiar with divorce, alcoholism, and tragedy. His mother was a product of a broken home and an alcoholic father. After several years of marriage, her first husband had died in an automobile accident, leaving her alone with two small children. A few years later, she remarried the owner of a successful construction company. The business was clearly the priority in their family life. And although my family had its share of dysfunction, at the end of the day what mattered most was always family—especially as it pertained to my dad.

Being a pregnant teenager brought great misgivings and fears for me—and for other family members as well, which they expressed all too often. But the first time my daughter, Vanessa, was placed in my arms, I immediately bonded with the tiny newborn nestling against my chest. My heart opened in a way that other mothers well understand. The relationship truly taught me the meaning of unconditional love. We were connected not only by a bloodline, but in spirit, too.

Despite the unsettling circumstances during this period in my life, my path to spiritual enlightenment took root. I began to pen my thoughts to paper, writing poems and short stories filled with emotions that I was unable to express otherwise. Before too long, the pen became my sword. With it, I waged a battle for my voice to be heard.

Over time, writing began to provide me with a sense of solace and I was able to find quiet contentment in the scripts I created. And so it seemed that once again, I was able to hear the angelic whispers being uttered in my ear. But this time, they were very different in tone. Instead of hearing words of guidance, I heard the pronouncements in the forms of poems and stories. As my creativity flourished, so did my spirit.

In some ways, writing allowed me to release the pent-up emotions that were trapped inside, and I could let them flow from my heart and mind to the pen held in my hand. The pen became the representative of the war going on within. Writing would later have a profound effect on my life, as it would turn out.

On the day of Vanessa's birth, I penned my first poem. Although I am unaware as to what prompted that action, I remember feeling a strong stirring inside my soul that urged me to write. As I did so, I felt my embattled mind ease. My inner voice was satisfied. Another gift from above. The poem was entitled "A Child Within a Child" and read:

A Child Within a Child

They tell me what I must be
They say I must begin to see
I see no tomorrows and no today
I see only the child within

I was a woman before I was a child
I carry a child within a child
A life soon destined to be
I am very young in mind
But yet, I pretend to be old
When will the woman in this youthful body emerge

I have no time for myself
Only for what I will bear
At times, I wish to enter my past
To find out where I decided to grow so fast
There I would linger for an eternity
Never wishing to grow old again

My lovely daughter started her life with some heavy weights to bear. As indicated, her birth was not much of a celebrated event. It was the early 1970s, and unwed pregnancies were far less common than they are today. At the time, most expectant teenagers were hidden away in disgrace, sent away to a distant relative until an adoption could be arranged, or pressured to marry the father. On top of this, the Catholic Church frowned upon premarital sex. In my case, its rebuke was swift, severe, and unmerciful. I had to spend several hours in front of priests and nuns, listening to how my actions were going to send me straight down into hellfire. Their words left a mark that made me feel tainted for many years to come. I felt branded in shame.

When I tell you that I knew the very moment Vanessa was conceived, believe me: it is a fact. Despite the limited knowledge of sex and my own reproductive system, I felt an instantaneous link to the universe when I became pregnant. It is a sensation of interconnectedness I find hard to describe. Over the years, I have heard many women indicate they, too, could feel life in their womb at the moment of conception. As the baby began to grow inside of me, I felt an immediate bond with her. Despite the negative judgments of church leaders and the emotional outbursts from my family members I had to endure, my heart was filled with love for that little girl growing inside my womb.

Vanessa's birth was not an easy one. She arrived five weeks earlier than the anticipated due date, weighing slightly over five pounds. Due to health complications, Vanessa had to remain in the hospital for two weeks after her birth. Yet, despite her medical issues, it was apparent she was determined to survive and thrive. When finally I could bring my little one home, that bond between mother and child flourished.

Vanessa grew into her adolescence through troubled times. After a few years of marriage, her dad became an alcoholic and our world as we knew it began to change. As the years passed by and his descent into addiction continued, Vanessa and I witnessed episodes of explosive violence. I desperately wanted to reach out and ask my parents for help, but I was so ashamed. I somehow felt that I was being punished by God for the pregnancy.

On the night I finally decided to leave my marriage, a violent argument ensued. My husband grabbed me by the throat until I almost lost consciousness. Somehow, I was able to grab a glass and metal ashtray to hit him with. He stumbled slightly and his hands lost their tight grip on my throat. Blood began to pour from his mouth and nose and he fell to the ground. As I watched him lying on the carpeted floor, I felt a calm take hold of me. I was no longer afraid. This was a turning point in my life. In the midst of all of the chaos, Vanessa walked into the bedroom and said, "Mommy, stop! Please stop fighting. It's time for us to leave."

In that moment, my heart broke for my little girl. She had witnessed all too much turmoil for such a young age. Although she appeared to be so small and frail in stature, her words were so wise and mature. They shocked me back into reality. So I took her hand in mine and we left the bedroom. With police sirens blaring in the background, I called my dad. That night, Vanessa slept in my parents' home. The next day, I moved back as well. When I left that January morning, I did not look back. I only looked forward to the peaceful reprieve of a safe haven.

The first months residing back in my parent's home were not an easy adjustment. However, despite the lack of room or privacy, it felt good to be with my family again. I had missed the noise of my younger siblings running through the house and calling out to one another. And, in the first few nights in my old bedroom, I became reacquainted with the concept of restful sleep. In that room, where I had grown up with my sisters and first saw the Archangel Michael, I found a peaceful reprieve from the past decade. In time, that peace allowed me to once again hear the whispers of the Archangel, who urged me to continue on my path.

Despite her father's negative behavior, Vanessa had remained a very caring child. She always seemed to have hope in her heart. In her innocent mind, she believed that someday her daddy would heal. In some ways, her hopefulness was a gift! Her optimistic outlook somehow brought out the smidgen of promise that remained inside of me.

As I look back on those early years of my daughter's life, I do so with great joy. To me, she was a blessing from the moment she arrived. With her, I found a new purpose for my being. Years later a relative once asked me, "Do you ever regret having your daughter?"

Before I responded, I looked over at Vanessa, who happened to be sitting right next to me. She began to fidget in anticipation of my response.

"There are no regrets with respect to the birth of my daughter. She grounded me and helped me to redirect my mind and my energies. She is the singular reason for my achievements."

As I finished uttering my words, I immediately looked over at Vanessa again; she was crying. When I reached to comfort her, she blurted out, "I'm so glad to know I didn't ruin your life when you decided to keep me. I've spent my life wondering if your choice to have me interfered with your future plans. When I see all that you have accomplished, I couldn't help but wonder how much more you would have achieved if you didn't have me when you were so young. Now that I know your true feelings, I feel much better about your decision to have me."

When Vanessa finished speaking, I reached over and embraced her. As I did, I could feel her body relax. I wiped away her tears, kissed her face, and said, "How could you have ever doubted that I wanted you? You were, and still remain, the bravest decision of my life."

Vanessa and I sat there in silence for a few moments. The dance between mother and child once again took place. Time seemed to stop as I reflected back on the sequence of my daughter's birth, to the initial moment when Vanessa first touched my chest with her tiny hand and synchronized my heart with hers. In the quiet of that hospital room long ago, I bonded with my baby girl. It is a bond like no other I have ever experienced.

And so, it seemed that once again, a blessing had been bestowed. As I watched Vanessa walk through her own front door later that night, she turned and waved. And for a moment, the image tugged at my heartstrings. Although she was no longer connected to me by the lifeline of an umbilical cord, she was indeed connected through the heartfelt sentiment between a mother and daughter. We were linked not only by genetic disposition, but by our souls, which had chosen to travel together in this lifetime. In her company, I have found an inner peace that could have been brought only by motherhood. It is a state of bliss that has enraptured my heart for all these years.

I have learned valuable lessons about life from each of the significant individuals who have shared a predominant part of my journey. But the most valuable lessons I have learned came through my relationship with Vanessa. From the moment I gave birth, I sensed an inner peace. A solace unlike any other that opened my mind to the meaning of motherhood and the infinite wisdom that comes with it. In serving as Vanessa's mom, I have learned the meaning of love in its purest sense. She gave me the opportunity to love her unconditionally, and for her to love me in the same manner. My daughter gave me the balance and the confidence to grow into the woman I am today.

To this day, I believe giving birth to Vanessa was indeed the bravest decision of my life. Somehow, even in my youthful state, I was capable of understanding the importance of bringing her precious life into the world. Perhaps it was the whispers of my angelic guides softly urging me to make the right decision. Whatever or whoever prompted me, I am grateful for the divine intercession; it helped me to make the best choice for us both. Vanessa's birth redefined me and remains my greatest blessing of all. It affirmed for me how very connected two souls can be.

CHAPTER 4

THE MAN FROM EIRE

*"You will find as you look back upon your life
that the moments that stand out, the moments
when you have really lived, are the moments when
you have done things in a spirit of love."*

~ HENRY DRUMMOND

After my marriage spiraled into a state of disrepair, I became acquainted with a fascinating older man. His name was Jamie, and he was an attorney by profession. He was highly educated, well-read, and quick-witted, too. He laughed easily and greatly enjoyed sharing a humorous story or a joke. We shared a love of books and he brought art and music back into my life. Additionally, he was of Irish heritage, and that gave me great delight.

For as many years as I can recall, I have been enamored with the lore of medieval history. As a little girl, I was beguiled by the tales of King Arthur, his knights of the Round Table, and stories of Camelot. I spent many an hour reading all about his noble adventures and gallant deeds. As I perused history books, my favorite chapters were always those about Irish culture. When possible, I would voraciously devour any book providing stories of the Druids, the High Kings of Tara, or those that depicted the lifestyle of the noble ladies and gents of yore. I would often daydream of castles and the stories they would tell if only the stone walls could talk. As I read about Celtic folklore, I dreamed of a handsome and dashing knight who would arrive at my doorstep, fall madly in love with me, and carry me off to a fortress by the sea. On occasion, I would conjure up visions of the past and wonder why I had such a fascination with Ireland. At times, my father would even remind me I was of Lebanese heritage and not of Irish descent. I would always retort, "Our Lebanese family has blue and green eyes. During the days of our Phoenician forefathers, someone must have snuck a Celt into the gene pool."

When I first met Jamie, he was a married man with a teenage daughter. Yet, despite my sense of propriety, I could not resist the temptation to love that man. As they say, the heart wants what the heart wants. I fell hard for Jamie and, when I was with him, my mind entered into a state of contentment that I had not experienced before. I began to flourish, and felt as if he had gifted me with a new life. For all too long, I had dreamed of being free from my husband's control. I craved the opportunity to become my own person and to explore all the possibilities the world offered. During this period of my life, I was quite pleased with the relationship because it gave me the best of both worlds. I had Jamie to depend on, but I also had my freedom. So, with my tumultuous marriage over, I sought refuge in a relationship with this gentle man whom I fondly nicknamed "Irishman." And in a very short time, I found solace in our mutual interests and in his willingness to shelter me. In my mind, the white knight had finally arrived in my life.

During the early stages of our relationship, Jamie lost his father, or "Da" as he had often referred to him. So as he grieved for his loss, he made arrangements to travel back to Ireland. He stopped by for a visit on his way to the airport. I expressed my condolences about his dad and listened to him as he shared some lovely stories about his childhood. Even though his tales often dealt with issues such as hardship and poverty, it was apparent he bore a genuine love for his dad and mom. When he spoke of his mother his eyes seemed to soften and he got a faraway look, as if reliving a special moment captured in his memory. What I gathered from his reminiscences was that he had shared a wonderful relationship with his parents. Since I, too, felt such a deep connection to my dad, I understood.

In time, Jamie and I found we had much common ground and we grew increasingly closer in our relationship. Once, as we were chatting about our lives, I saw an apparition of an older woman appear. Her build was brawny, but her features were pleasant. She had dark hair that was laced with gray, worn in a twisted ponytail. The woman wore a light brown cotton dress with printed flowers on it and a mustard yellow sweater. The sleeves of the knitted garment were pulled up around her elbows. As Jamie continued to describe his family's homestead, I could see the woman looking at him in an admiring manner. He grinned and explained that the woman fit his mother's description. To my surprise, he didn't seem astonished by this; on the contrary, he seemed comforted. Jamie even went as far as to say that his mother could see apparitions, too. Whenever he and I talked about matters of the spirit, it was amazing to me how comfortable he seemed to be with the topic. For a short time, Jamie's mother remained in the room, smiling silently. Somehow, I could sense her pride in her son, and at one point I thought I even heard her whisper his name.

When Jamie left for Ireland, I sensed a vulnerability in him—something I had not observed in him before. He seemed most distraught about not having had the opportunity to express a proper good-bye to his father. After Jamie departed for the airport, I couldn't quite get him off my mind. As the days passed, I found myself continuously thinking of him. During the nights, I had a recurring dream about him and his family. I visualized all of them walking up a beautiful, scenic green hill with a casket set upon their shoulders. There were numerous men slowly climbing up the picturesque hillside with others trailing behind. In the vision, I could also see Jamie placing the most beautiful, soft-toned, peach-hued roses onto his father's grave. As he stood at the grave site, I visualized tears streaming down his face. The tears seemed to trail down to the very ground where his dad had been laid to rest. At times, the dream felt so real: I could actually smell the lovely fragrance of the rosebuds. And, on one particular night, I heard a whisper, "Gift him with roses in this color."

As part of my preparations to welcome Jamie back home, I ordered a dozen peach-hued roses and brought them to his office. On the day of his return, I placed the flowers on his desk. With tears in his eyes he inquired, "How did you know the color of the roses I placed on my dad's grave?"

I told him about the recurring dream I had been experiencing. He in turn informed me that my description was an exact depiction of the actual event. We looked at each other for a few minutes, saying nothing. But once again,

I wondered about the eerie connection that somehow linked us.

It seemed he and I were so very connected, in both mind and spirit. It somehow felt as if we were kindred souls. We could truly finish each other's sentences. I recall one night in particular. I was working, but I suddenly felt his presence. The impression was so vivid, I knew instantly that he was not well. I sensed he was having trouble breathing and that his heart was racing. I started to panic; I was sure he was having a heart attack. I called him, but there was no answer. A few hours later, he called to tell me that he had been to the hospital due to an angina attack. The doctors were sure he was going to be all right, but cautioned him about reducing his stress. As I lay in bed that night, I felt him so close and knew that he was thinking of me.

A few months later, my father took me aside and lectured me about the situation. "He is a married man, Lillie," Dad said, "and he has a child. I raised you better than this."

As he voiced his opinion, I could see the hurt and worry in Dad's eyes. His comments wrenched my heart. I knew I had disappointed my parents years before, when I became pregnant as a teen. And even though I knew they didn't blame me when my marriage failed, I knew they were equally upset with the present situation.

A few days later I told Jamie I had to end our relationship. As I left Jamie's office, I gently kissed his lips and traced the lines of his face. I did so to etch his features in my memory.

Some months passed, and my feelings for Jamie were unchanged. I missed him immensely and longed for us to be together again. The spark he had ignited inside my heart seemed to dwindle without his constant presence. One evening after a very long day at work, I arrived home feeling distraught. To my surprise, I saw a long, narrow, white box on the kitchen table. The package was addressed to me, and was clearly filled with flowers—there were green stems protruding from the bottom. As I gently opened the box, my eyes filled with tears at the sight of lovely, soft, peach roses. They were so beautiful and fragrant. Attached to one of the roses was a card containing a message:

I have moved and this is my address and telephone number. Please come soon, Irishman.

As I read those few words in silence, my heart leapt and my mind raced. I found myself picking up the telephone and dialing his number. The moment I heard him respond on the other end of the receiver, I began to cry with joy. As he said my name my heart flipped and I knew it would be just minutes before he and I could be together again. I ran from the house to my car and drove straight to his new home. As he stepped onto the porch to greet me, I jumped into his arms. We spent one of the most romantic nights I have ever experienced. It was a night of sheer elegance. That night, I believe I finally emerged as a woman. I opened up my heart, and my mind expanded from experiencing a deep and binding love that was filled with sensuality and grace. Over the next few years, we shared a wonderful relationship. It was a time of great joy and discovery, but was intermixed with some disappointment and sadness as well. In his arms, I found a sense of myself that remains with me until this very day.

CHAPTER 5

MEMORIES OF THE IRISH SEA

My relationship with Jamie afforded me opportunities to travel to Ireland. During these trips, Vanessa would stay with my parents. I was grateful to know she was safe in their company, and that allowed me to feel more at ease about the journey across the sea.

When we did visit, it was a time of sheer magic for me. The lure to this mystical land was so strong. On my first days in the land of forty shades of green, my soul seemed to find its homeland. As I stood on the cliffs above Slea Head Beach on the Dingle Peninsula, my body, mind, and soul fully embraced the land and the sea. With the misty ocean spray stinging my face and the wind ripping through my hair, I felt both alive and inspired. I felt the rise of a higher self slowly reawaken. In standing on that precipice, I could almost imagine the Spanish Armada ships as they raced toward the coastline and became submerged by the rough waters of the sea. I could envision the Spanish warriors being washed ashore half-drowned and exhausted, crawling toward land. I could hear my inner call of the wild emerge as my Phoenician ancestors cried out to me and reminded me of our past seafaring days. And when Jamie and I roamed palatial castles in Dublin or Waterford, or ancient ruins where kings had once stood, my heart and soul were at peace. My spirit traveled to a distant time where it had first felt solace reign. I was home, and every part of me knew it to be fact.

On our first night on the Emerald Isle, we stayed at a bed-and-breakfast on the southwestern coast. It was located near a bird sanctuary. As I walked to the banks of a nearby tributary, the feel of the land and the smell of the air called to my soul. My spirit danced at the scenery and seemed to lift from within. I felt exhilarated, a sensation that was incomparable to feelings in my past travels. The look of the thatch-roof homes and the smell of the peat burning in the parlor's fireplace were indescribable, yet, somehow familiar to me. Each new place we visited gave me a feeling of déjà vu. All the sites and sounds were recognizable and pleasing to me. It felt like a homecoming of the soul as I traveled over the soil of Eire.

On this, my initial visit to Ireland, we had the opportunity to tour Dromoland Castle. I credit this visit as the catalyst for my current belief in reincarnation. I had waited for so long to tour the castle and the grounds around it, too. The land where the castle now stood once housed the O'Brien clan and their homestead. The O'Briens are of the lineage of my favorite of the high kings: Brian Boru. I had spent many a day reading the tales of him and his final battle at Clontarf. I had waited for so long to walk in the very steps of his ancestors, to look at the inside of the castle, to gaze upon the furnishings, the books, and the paintings, and to touch the stones of the walls. I had also awaited the chance to place my ear against the huge stone walls and to listen to the whispers and ancient secrets contained inside their granite and carved marble. I longed to see the outside grounds as well, and to touch a gazebo I had read about that had stood in its place for hundreds of years.

After admiring the exterior of the castle, we decided to look at the outbuildings and gardens on the castle's grounds, and began walking down the pathway toward the gazebo. The path itself was lined with trees that looked as if they should be used in a scene from a Gothic horror film: they looked ancient, their bark was dark in color, and Spanish moss hung from their branches. The moss appeared to have a life of its own and seemed to reach down toward the path, as if it were trying to grab those strolling beneath its tentacles. As we approached the gazebo area, my senses seemed to become more aroused to the sounds and smells. And my mind seemed to become more aware of the surroundings.

I stopped when I heard what I thought to be the buzzing sound of many bees. "What's wrong?" Jamie asked.

"Do you hear the bees?" I replied.

Jamie looked at me in a perplexed manner and continued to walk forward. Although I was a bit confused by what I was hearing I, too, continued on the path. The sound intensified and I began to feel dizzy. Before I could rebalance my senses, I heard what I thought were people crying out in pain.

With the next step, a flash of light blazed before my eyes and I saw what appeared to be a battle scene taking place in front of me. The apparition looked to be a scene from the medieval times. I saw the men striking one another with swords. I saw knights wearing helmets and chain-mail armor. I smelled smoke and blood and heard the cries of the injured as they lay on the ground, crippled with pain. Then I saw a woman lying on the ground. She was bleeding from her stomach and appeared to be dead;

there were no signs of life. By her side stood a man. He was wearing the same chain-mail armor, but his helmet had been removed. He stood hunched over and was leaning on a lengthy sword. He was a strikingly handsome man with long, dark-blond hair. He had sculpted facial features and was tall, with broad shoulders. He seemed to be very distraught at the sight of the woman, and tears were running down his face. As I looked even closer at the scene, my eyes caught on the woman's long red hair and her face. I strained my eyes to try and see her more clearly—her features were a mirror image of my own. With this first look of recognition, I felt my heart stop, and my breath froze in my lungs. What did this mean? Was this place so familiar to me because of some past-life experience? As the thoughts whirled inside my head, I quickly became disoriented and fainted.

When I came to, I found myself lying on the castle's exterior stairwell. Jamie was kneeling next to me, and several strangers were standing around as well.

I looked up at him. "What happened?"

"You fainted," he said.

I tried to refocus on him and on the immediate surroundings. But try as I might, I kept seeing the battle scene repeatedly playing in my mind. I made an attempt to explain the experience to Jamie, but he would not hear of it. He insisted my overactive imagination had mixed with the heat of the day and I was suffering from some sort of sunstroke.

When I could finally rise to my feet, we began to make our way toward the castle. Once again, I froze in my steps. I turned toward him and said, "I can't stay in that castle tonight! Don't you know that is where I died?"

As I uttered the words, my mind again transcended to that time long ago. I saw a lovely, redheaded maiden laid to rest in the castle. She was dressed in an emerald gown and placed on a cold slab of marble for all to view. She was mourned by many, but most especially by a handsome man I knew must have been her husband. I stood on the exterior stairwell of Dromoland Castle as these memories flitted across the sky in front of me. Jamie just kept looking at me in disbelief. He muttered a few more comments about my imagination. Yet, despite his protests, deep inside I knew the truth. My memory had regressed to a past life and I immediately understood why I felt so drawn to the Emerald Isle. It was a feeling of pure connection to the people, to the land, and to the sea. That afternoon, we left the castle and its lavish grounds and found refuge that evening in a bed-and-breakfast a few miles up the road. As we drove away from the mighty fortress, I couldn't help but feel I had once again left a part of myself behind.

Upon my return home, I spent time telling my parents about all the places we had visited and all the sights of Ireland. I described the various locations, the ocean, and most especially the castles. They listened intently and were amused by my descriptions and stories. After I shared my experience at Dromoland Castle, I inquired if either of them believed in reincarnation. My mother reacted in her normal manner and immediately responded she did not believe in such nonsense and that the Catholic Church frowned upon the concept of reincarnation. My dad, on the other hand, indicated otherwise. Although he didn't personally believe in more than one life for each of us, he was familiar with books that indicated the Catholic Church had permitted its followers to believe in reincarnation in the early days of its formation. Dad's comments gave rise to my curiosity, and I began to explore the concept of past lives. In researching my experience and others', I came to believe that a soul can indeed be reincarnated.

As time passed, my romance with the Irishman became very strained. And as much as I treasured Jamie and our trips together, our relationship could not withstand time. For whatever reasons, my mind became tormented by a kaleidoscope of events that had lain hidden in my sub-conscious for far too long. The loving relationship we once shared turned into an emotional tug-of-war. Jamie would move forward, and I would move backward. When he was ready to commit, I was not.

As I revisit the many sequences of my life, I know my fondness for Jamie, and for Ireland, will never change. I am keenly aware that my love for each dwells inside a special part of my heart. In my recollections of our time together, I have created a requiem for my love of him. It is a distant drum of life that continues to have a hold on me, and has never faded from my view.

Looking back, I am now aware of why Jamie was cho-sen to become a part of my life. It was not only because of heartfelt sentiment or physical attraction: it was for the purpose of protecting my soul. Like the Archangel Michael, who I trust to guard me, I chose a man I believed was capable of shielding me in this earthly domain. Not just my physical being, but my spirit as well. So in essence, our relationship helped me learn to lower the tough exte-rior I often project and to embrace the gentle spirit within.

When I listen to my favorite Celtic songs, I long to smell the Irish Sea, to listen to the waves as they crash against the coastal rocks, to walk the mountains and the green fields of Eire. It is my hope that someday in the near future, Jamie and I will travel again to my spiritual homeland across the ocean. A place where our souls are joined as one. For I am convinced that, somewhere out there, in the land where the Druids once roamed and the dolmen stones stand erect as the early morning mist rises from the ground, lie the remains of my body from a past life long ago.

As I reminisced on the night of a full moon about the Emerald Isle, I heard words softly whispered in my ear. As usual, I penned the utterances to page. And I came to realize that a lovely verse had been created about my deep connection to the land of Eire.

Let Me Go Home

Let me go home Lord to the sweet surrender of the Emerald Isle.

Let me go back to the brilliant twinkling light of my soul's repose.

Let my arrival be laced with the enduring elegance and grace of a moonlit night.

Let me sit on the Irish cliffs of Moher and there ever watchful in silence to dwell.

As the waves strike and reinvigorate my being, I will place my mind in rhythm with the sea.

For this is the one place that I can sit and hear the voices of the angels.

It is here that I feel free to whisper my prayers in rejoice.

In its seclusion, is the stay of memory Divine and the opening to Heaven's gate as it remains.

The recollections of long ago are restored with each movement of the wild Celtic sea.

As the everlasting waves move in time with each heartbeat, I will walk across the green fields among the aromatic roses and heather blooms.

Let me go home Lord to revitalize my soul.
Let me go home Lord to prepare for the peaceful journey to the light.
Let me go home Lord forever more, for ever more and a day.

CHAPTER 6

FIRST TOUR OF DUTY

The many lessons that I have learned in this lifetime have not come easily. My chosen path has not always helped me to evolve into a better person or benefited my spiritual growth. But I believe that one particular decision helped me understand what it truly means to serve. When I chose to join the ranks of the law enforcement profession, it was in some way, the beginning of the rest of my life. When I signed on, I began a journey that impacted both my humanity and my spirituality, too. As I look back at this extraordinary event, I am both humbled and pleased in my decision.

In the early summer of 1984, an unexpected opportunity presented itself. The local police department posted that it was accepting applications for the position of a patrol officer. When I initially heard about the job opening, I was very intrigued by the prospect. I had always been interested in law enforcement, but had not pursued it due to my responsibilities as a wife and mother. So after contemplating the possibility, I eagerly applied and went through the physical fitness test, written exam, and several oral interviews. Soon after, I was appointed the first female police officer in the city of Arnold, Pennsylvania.

My first tour of duty arrived on September 16, 1984. As I prepared for the day, I recall walking over to the mirror to see myself wearing a uniform for the first time. My, how the image had changed! I turned toward the window and looked down over the community, the river that flowed across the lower valley, and the very streets that I would soon be patrolling. I worried most about the areas located beyond the boundaries of the railroad tracks because the neighborhood had changed for the worse. When I was a little girl, those streets had been a safe place to play with all the other children in the neighborhood. The area had since become barely recognizable. The crime rate had dramatically increased and the homes had become run-down. The once-familiar playground had turned into a war zone of violent acts, drug dealers, and other criminals. I would now be responsible for serving and protecting the residents of the community. I only hoped that I was prepared to tackle the challenges that lay ahead. Unknown to me at the time, my baptism by fire was about to commence.

My thoughts soon returned to the present business of that day, and I realized that in just a few minutes I would need to report. I started combing my hair and applying makeup in an effort to look more feminine, since every piece of clothing I had on was tailored to fit a man. When I was about finished getting ready, I grabbed the gun belt and wrapped it over the top of my pants. I attempted to snap it in place, but it would not clasp shut. I became frustrated and swore out loud.

At that very second, my mother arrived at my bedroom door and asked, "Who are you swearing at?"

I responded, "My damn gun belt."

At my response, Mom shook her head and promptly left the room, mumbling something about my vulgar language. As I made another attempt to fasten the gun belt, I glanced at my watch. I realized my patrol partner would be arriving shortly, so I grabbed my gear and headed down the stairs. As I walked out the door and onto the front porch, I had my head lowered and I was not paying attention to my surroundings. When I looked up, I saw a police officer standing there next to my mother.

He looked at me, smiled, and said, "Your mother tells me that you're having trouble fastening your gun belt. She yelled for me to come up here and see if I could assist you with your problem."

When he finished speaking, I could feel my face grow warm. I was so embarrassed—and I could only imagine how flushed my cheeks were. As I walked toward him with my gun belt in hand, I glared angrily at Mom. I was mortified. As he fastened the gun belt, he quietly said, "Everyone has a tough time with their gun belt at first. They are so stiff and they barely budge, much less fasten. It'll take a few weeks before it gets easier. I won't tell anyone about this and, if you don't, it will be just our secret."

However, his promise about keeping it a private matter did not last. The gun-belt scenario became a part of how he regularly introduced me to fellow officers. As time went on, I realized that his comments were not made in mockery, but in pride. In my heart I knew he was pleased to have been a part of helping me learn the ropes. Although he was a few years younger than I, we knew one another socially. He had gone to school and played football with my brothers. I had also become acquainted with him in a business capacity. During the last years of my marriage, I had owned a small restaurant in the community and the Arnold police officers routinely stopped by the shop during foot patrols of the business district. When I separated from my husband, the officers would occasionally drive me home late at night after I closed the restaurant.

When my patrol partner finished fastening my gun belt, he patted me on the shoulder and asked me if I was ready to go. I nodded my head and quietly uttered, "Yes."

As I was about to turn away, I looked back at my dad and smiled. "I'll see you tonight," I said.

He looked at me and replied, "Be careful."

Again, I smiled and turned to follow my partner to the car. Before I stepped off the porch, Dad said, "Girl, come back up here for a minute. I have something to say."

Dad placed my hand in his and led me inside the house. He then said, "Girl, I know that you are a grown woman. However, as your father I'll support your choice as long as you remember a few things. First, always remember you are a woman. Never forget: your femininity is what makes you so special. If you start behaving like a man, I expect you to quit this job. Second, don't ever be so stupid as to not be afraid, but don't ever be so afraid you can't do your job. I want you to remember that through the grace of God and the fact that you had good parents, you are where you are in this life. So don't judge others. And don't embarrass yourself; if you do, you disgrace the family name as well. If you promise to abide by these rules, I'll stand behind you one hundred percent. But if you fail to remember what I have told you today, I'll demand you quit your job. Do you understand all that I have said, girl?"

I nodded my head and simply responded, "Yes."

I walked over to my father and kissed the top of his head. He pulled me to him and hugged me. I could sense his worry and fear for me. He took his hand and placed a tiny sign of the cross on my head. It was a gesture he had repeated with all of us children since our births. I turned to walk out the door, but stopped in front of the statue of the Blessed Mother and genuflected. I rose, kissed the statue, and whispered a silent prayer for protection on my first tour of duty. All at once, I felt tears begin to form in my eyes and blinked them away. As I walked out of the house, I turned to look once more at Dad. He just sat there, smiling at me. It was a smile that I would remember for the rest of my life.

With all of the hope I held about the task I was on my way to undertake, my mind was having a hard time grasping the meaning of Dad's words. However, in the years to come, his statements would really resonate. Any time I felt myself judging another's lifestyle, I would hear his voice echoing in my ear. Dad had instilled a sense of what being a good police officer would mean. Wearing the blue meant finding a balanced approach to addressing difficult situations, even as I worked to protect my community and fellow officers, too.

As I slowly walked down the sidewalk and got in the patrol car, my partner looked intently at me and smiled. "Are you ready to roll?" he asked.

Reluctantly, I said, "Let's go."

As we pulled away from the house, I looked at the man sitting next to me in the car, smiled broadly, and took a deep breath. I turned my head to look forward and felt myself shaking inside with the adrenaline of the moment. I found it hard to contain my excitement and simultaneously quash the fear I felt. Every part of my mind began to scream a silent warning. I almost yelled at him to turn the car around! Just as I was about to, a calm came over me and my spirit took control. I heard the soft whispers of my angelic guide as he reassured me: "All is well."

As my mind quieted, I reminded myself that this was the day I had been looking forward to. This would be my day in the sun—my moment to shine. Soon, the dispatcher's voice crackled over the radio, and a sense of pride filled my being. I buried my fear somewhere within and ventured into uncharted territory.

For over 25 years, I served in the law enforcement profession. Each and every day, I attempted to live up to my promise to my dad. Although, like most people, I have some regrets, in the end I still believe I made the right decision in choosing my career path. If I had the opportunity to do it all again, I would make the same choice, and without any hesitation. My days wearing the blue taught me a great deal about life. They helped me begin to see how clearly we are all intrinsically linked, physically and spiritually. I learned how one positive act of kindness or negative action can alter the greater good of us all. Through this, I blossomed into a competent civil servant who learned to trust her instincts—and the Archangel's whispered guidance.

CHAPTER 7

HEY, LITTLE GIRL

As time passed, I felt as if I was riding on a roller coaster. My life seemed to be in a state of perpetual motion. I tried to balance being a good mom and police officer. As the days swiftly progressed, I met so many other law enforcement officers, dispatchers, firefighters, and emergency service personnel as well. It seemed everyone wanted to meet the woman who dared to defy the odds by becoming the community's first female police officer. Many residents expressed their delight and surprise when they saw me on duty. It appeared I was the new town novelty—or perhaps the pariah they all wanted to catch a glimpse of.

One particular individual voiced his opinion about me on a quiet midnight shift when my patrol partner and I made a stop at a neighboring police department. As we walked into the station, I noticed on older man sitting behind the glass partition. He was smoking a cigarette, and the smoke filled his cubicle. It seemed to linger above his head like a cloud. As I watched him, I immediately thought of an old black-and-white film noir, in which a detective sat in a small smoky room with the venetian blinds pulled down, interrogating a suspect.

Within moments I was introduced to this man, Frank. He appeared to be giving me a once-over. I instantly felt a bit uncomfortable. He stared at me silently. When he finally spoke, he asked me to come closer so he could get a better look at me. Although I was taken aback, I did so out of respect. As I inched closer, he motioned for me to turn sideways. Once again, I did as he asked. Without missing a beat, he inhaled on his cigarette as if to add extra drama to his next words. Then, with a sly grin on his face, he uttered, "Hey, little girl, does your daddy know you're carrying a gun?"

He then sat back in his chair with a wicked grin plastered across his face. He seemed pleased with his comment and smug in his anticipation of my reply. So as not to disappoint, I immediately chirped back, "Yes, he does. And as a matter of fact, he taught me how to shoot it, too."

I returned the smile and awaited his response to my retort. After a moment of awkward silence, his mouth turned up into a mischievous smile and his eyes twinkled. He looked like a little boy who had just pulled off a marvelous prank. Within a few seconds, his smirk turned into laughter. Soon all three of us were laughing out loud. It was in that moment I knew I had won over this jovial man. It seemed I had found a friend and forged an alliance that was built on mutual respect. And although we initially shared different viewpoints on women serving in law enforcement, we both learned to respect each other's opinions. In time, Frank would confide that he was proud to have lived long enough to see women serving in a vocation that he once considered a proving ground for men only. Those words caused a sense of pride to well up within me.

As the weeks swiftly passed by, I worked tirelessly to learn about department policies, procedures, and my fellow officers. Having no past experience in law enforcement, it was an arduous task to undertake. I also trained in martial arts and bodybuilding in order to strengthen myself physically and mentally. Over time, I developed a strong sense of self-confidence.

Yet, despite my hard work and willingness to learn, I made a few errors along the way. Like the first time I tried to use the patrol car radio. The system did not operate at all how I had expected. After weeks of listening to the back-and-forth banter, I felt sure I was prepared to use it. So one otherwise quiet evening, an emergency domestic disturbance call was dispatched. I listened intently to all of the details as they were relayed. With the excitement of a child who is handed a new toy, I picked up the microphone and said, "Ten-four."

Within seconds, I heard some static come across the radio. A few more seconds passed and I heard one of the male officers say, "There must be something wrong with the radio. I swear I just heard a squeak coming from it. It sounded like Minnie Mouse was talking."

All at once, I heard laughter roll across the airwaves. One officer after the other repeated the words about the so-called squeak in the radio. I looked at my partner, who was doing his best not to laugh. He, too, soon erupted into uncontrollable laughter. I felt my face flush in embarrassment. I turned again toward my partner and gave him one of *those* female stares—the kind known to strike fear in any man.

The next few minutes, as we drove in the direction of the emergency call, the laughter continued among my male counterparts. Upon our arrival at the scene, I picked up the mic again and informed the dispatcher. To my surprise, one of the officers complained again about the "squeak" in his radio. This time, however, I chose to ignore the comment and concentrated on responding to the call. Once on scene, the jovial banter ceased and all of the officers focused their attention on the situation at hand.

Over the next few days, I became the brunt of all too many jokes about my mouselike voice. However, within a short period of time, the men learned if they dished it out, they had better be prepared to take it. After all, I had been raised with five brothers!

In the years that followed my initiation, this type of lighthearted ribbing continued. I learned that it was the common language in my new world, and was not just directed at me. On all too many occasions, we used teasing or pranks to dissipate the stress caused by an incident. To a civilian, such boisterous dialogue might have sounded harsh, but for those of us wearing the blue it was simply part of our way of life. It helped ease fears and release the tension that our jobs brought, and in some way served as a means of healing.

CHAPTER 8

MOTHER TERESA IN UNIFORM

"I want you to remember that through the grace of God and the fact that you had good parents, you are where you are in this life . . . don't judge others."

It wasn't long before Dad's advice proved useful. I had been working in the field only a few months before I truly understood what he meant. One early experience had such a profound impact on me that it left a permanent impression and influenced the way I would serve the greater good afterward.

The chief had directed all officers to monitor the southern end of town and to keep an eye out for any criminal activity while conducting routine patrols. Complaints received from residents indicated there had been problems with prostitution in the neighborhood recently. Up until that point, I had very limited firsthand knowledge about life on the street, especially as it concerned the "ladies of the evening." Having married quite early, my life had been somewhat sheltered.

On one particular evening, I noticed a woman hail down a car and then lean over to talk to the driver. After a brief discussion, she got in the car. Noticing this suspicious behavior, I followed them. When the vehicle stopped, I sat watching as their shadows began to move. I called for backup. In just a few moments, my partner arrived and we quietly approached the vehicle. As soon as we knocked on the window and aimed our flashlights inside the car, it became apparent what was going on. As I peered at the two of them and caught sight of their half-naked bodies, I became embarrassed.

My partner ordered the man and woman to get out of the car. As the man stepped out, zipping his pants, he tearfully began to confess that he was married. The woman exited and showed no emotion. She had also somehow managed to fully dress herself within seconds. As she stood there on that cold, wintry night, I realized that she did not have much clothing on: a short-sleeved T-shirt, a hooded jacket that zipped, a pair of cut-off blue jean shorts, and flip-flop sandals. I was perplexed by her summerlike apparel, but I tried to focus on my duties. The pair were then placed in handcuffs and transported to the police department for processing.

At the station, my partner wrote the male a citation and let him go. When I asked him why he had cut the man loose but arrested the prostitute, he said, "It was the man's first offense; the woman has a longstanding criminal history for both drug dealing and prostitution."

I reminded him that, according to Pennsylvania law, both parties were equally guilty in this scenario. When I accused my partner of bias, he just shrugged his shoulders and walked away. I turned my focus back to the woman, finished processing her, and placed her in a holding cell. I could sense a deep sadness in her, and her demeanor somehow made me feel uncomfortable—a sensation I had not felt before in the course of my duties. Before I left, she asked if she could make a phone call. She explained that she needed to make arrangements for someone to babysit her children overnight. My heart fell. I promptly gave her the chance to do so.

A few minutes later, the woman was back inside the cell and sitting on a thin, stained mattress atop a cold metal slab; that would have to serve as her bed for the night. When I went to lock the iron gate on her, I again hesitated for a minute. I wanted to give her some words of advice, but the look on her face made me refrain. As I turned to leave, I stopped and asked, "What are you doing dressed like that in the middle of winter? Don't you know it is cold outside?"

She looked up at me with her sad brown eyes and replied, "Do you think I would be outside doing what I do if I could afford clothes for me and food for my kids?"

Until that moment, it hadn't dawned on me how fortunate I had been in my own life. This poor woman clearly had had a rough life. I felt so foolish.

As I left the cell, I realized what I needed to do. Later that evening, I went to my home and grabbed a box of brand-new loafers from my closet. I had only recently purchased them, so they were unworn. On my way back to the police station, I stopped at a local department store and purchased a couple of pairs of socks.

A short time later, I returned to the station and went into the cell to check on the woman. Before exiting, I said, "When you make bail, there will be a pair of shoes and some socks for you to take."

At that moment, she looked up at me, her eyes filled with tears. I was about to ask her why she was crying, but she turned her head away from me. I knew instinctively I should not pry any further, so I just left the cell. Then I realized I was also shedding tears. To this day, I wish I would have said more to her in her moment of pain. Maybe I could have uttered something positive that would have convinced her to alter her lifestyle. But in my first few months as a rookie cop, I was not very savvy; that came in later years. However, in offering the shoes to that downtrodden women, I began to trust the intuitive gift that dwelled inside my being. I believe that the angel whispered to me and instructed me to make a small gesture of kindness, and that this affirmed for her that there *were* individuals out there who still embraced humanity.

Over the next few years, the woman and I would occasionally cross paths. Sometimes it was when I was arresting her for a crime that she had committed. Other times, I would see her at community events. When I learned that she succumbed to an illness several years later, I felt remorse for never having had the opportunity to talk with her in private again. I was grateful, however, to have had the chance to aid her in some small way. The experience helped me realize that I needed to serve and protect others without passing judgment. I began to grow into the police officer my dad had hoped I would become.

As a result of this encounter, my colleagues dubbed me "Mother Teresa in Uniform." By extending one simple act of compassion, I had been canonized as the local patron saint of streetwalkers. This nickname was often quipped at me by my fellow officers when I extended a hand to others. Despite their sarcasm, I embraced it. To be deemed empathetic in any degree is an honor. It would be a privilege to have lived my life in some minor reflection of the real Mother Teresa's. Even though she wore a habit, I consider her a fellow "first responder" who wore her uniform well.

She set such an example of humility and kindness for all to follow. She emanated such piety and grace toward the people that she served while patrolling the streets of Calcutta. On her careful watch, all of humanity was graced. Mother Teresa left the earth with such a miraculous legacy of integrity. Someday, I aspire to leave my mark on humanity, too. Through my work, I pray that I have provided a simple contribution to better the life of at least one of God's children. In doing so, I believe I have honored both fathers—the heavenly one who beckoned me to serve, and the earthly one who provided guidance about serving. On the day that my soul enters the spirit world, I pray I will be welcomed home and hear the words, "Well done, my daughter."

CHAPTER 9

MY DAYS
WEARING THE BLUE

My days wearing the blue were some of the happiest and proudest moments in my life. In the police profession, I found my calling and believed I had answered God's call to service. The thrill of it all still exhilarates me!

At the time of my hiring, Pennsylvania law permitted a police officer to serve in the field before attending the police academy, which I finally did after some six months on the job. On the first day of training, I stood in formation as the only female in a sea of men. And due to the fact that I wore eye makeup, the drill sergeant nicknamed me "Cleopatra."

I attended the academy on a grueling schedule of study and competition. Being the only woman in the class only added to the stress, and the long hours I had to spend there didn't help ease Vanessa's apprehension about my chosen profession. When I returned home in the evenings, many hours were spent studying for the oral and written exams. It was fortunate that we were still living with my parents.

After graduating from the academy, I went back to work on the streets. Like most rookie cops, I made a multitude of mistakes that required some additional intervention by veteran officers. Thank God, they were not errors that caused any real grief to any of the parties involved! In my fellow officers, I found both friends and enemies. The initial eighteen months of my career were a literal "baptism by fire." It took a great deal of determination and patience to prove myself. With each passing day, my confidence increased. A sense of pride gradually permeated my being. It finally felt as if I had found my purpose.

I remember one of the first calls I responded to without any backup. It was a burglary in progress. When I arrived at the scene, there was an elderly woman standing outside of her home yelling, "There is a man inside my house!"

My training kicked in, and I leapt to action and entered the home. I placed the cold steel of my service revolver in my hands and carefully entered the residence. I searched each room, but the intruder was already gone. Evidently, he fled out the same window he had used to enter the home. Once the entire house was checked and secured, I went back outside. The neighbors had by then gathered around the poor woman. I tried to calm her down and asked her a few questions about what happened. As I stood there awaiting her reply, she looked at me in quite a bewildered manner.

"I don't want you—I want the real police."

I was perplexed by her comment. "I *am* the real police," I said.

"No, you're not! I want a male officer to help me. Women can't be police officers."

I guessed her to be around 80 years of age. Obviously, she was from a different era and a bit set in her ways. In that moment, I realized I had a choice to make. Either I could feel insulted by her remarks, or I could set my feeling aside and try to ease her distress.

"The men are all busy right now so they sent me instead. Why don't you give me a chance to help you? If I can't do the job, I'll call one of the men to assist you," I said.

When I finished speaking, she half-smiled and nodded her head in agreement. She invited me into her home for a cup of tea and we continued talking about the incident. As the teapot brewed, she searched the house to determine whether the burglar had taken any of her prized possessions. Over the warm tea, we chatted and she reminisced about her life and all of the changes she had witnessed. She spoke of our town's "good old days" and seemed saddened by its recent decline. When I moved to leave her home that morning, she grabbed my hand.

"Honey, you're right. You *are* the real police. You did a nice job today. You hang in there, and don't let anybody tell you that you can't do this job," she said.

I thanked her and left. As I drove away, I knew that something had changed inside of me. That event strengthened my resolve and confirmed that I had indeed chosen a good career path for myself.

In the months that followed, the chief requested that I work the investigations of crimes against children. He believed that I might be able to bring a more caring approach to those traumatic situations than some of the other officers. I gathered his decision had to do with the fact that I was not only a woman, but a mother as well.

Within days of this conversation with the chief, I was assigned my first case. Whenever there was a report of suspected child abuse, the children's bureau personnel would arrive at the police station and advise the on-duty officers about the complaint received. It was then the responsibility of the officers to transport the caseworker to the home where the incident had been reported. The caseworker would enter the residence and conduct a preliminary inquiry. If for some reason he or she felt a child was in imminent danger, the officer was required to intervene, contact the judge on call, and take immediate custody of the minor.

On that particular day, the caseworker had received a complaint regarding an infant who had not been seen or heard for a few days. The complainant feared something might have been wrong with the child because she had heard the parents arguing, but no sounds from the baby. Just a few minutes after the caseworker had entered the home, she came back out and appeared to be quite distressed. She asked me to contact the judge immediately, and then relayed the details of her observations. When she had asked the parents if she could see the baby, both of them refused. When the caseworker insisted and indicated that a police officer was waiting outside, the parents complied. A first glance into the crib revealed a baby boy who had obvious injuries. The child looked as if he had several broken limbs, and there were burn marks on his body. As a means of keeping the child from crying out, a cloth rag had been stuffed inside his mouth. When she finished describing the circumstances, I felt my emotions flare. For a moment, I felt it would be nearly impossible to contain the surge of anger that welled inside me. I immediately contacted the dispatcher and relayed the information. I requested the administrative judge be contacted, and asked for medical personnel and additional officers at the scene.

Within minutes, backup arrived and we entered the house. We placed both parents under arrest. The caseworker wrapped the little boy in a blanket and gently lifted him from the crib. When she did, the infant cried out in pain. It took everything in me to stay focused on the tasks at hand. The baby was taken to the waiting ambulance and driven to the hospital. As the other officers and I put the parents in the back of the patrol car, I couldn't help but feel a strong urge to hurt them. It took every bit of self-restraint I had not to. When we arrived at the station, we locked the parents in their cells. As all of this was happening, I kept hearing the words my dad used to say about my siblings and me: *"My children are my gold and silver."* And I wondered why that little boy's parents didn't perceive him as their gold or silver.

After that incident, I wasn't quite sure if the chief had been right to appoint me to work in that new role. I didn't believe either of us had considered how damaging it would be to my mother's heart or the lasting effect it would have on me. To this day, I still think about that precious baby boy, as I have about many other sad memories as well. It was on those first days working with the children, though, that I became aware of why God had sent me on this journey.

In March 1986, I would go on to develop and manage the crime-prevention programs for the department and finally find my niche. That forum provided me with the opportunity to spend time with the residents of the community, strategizing ways to prevent and reduce crime. This was a positive, uplifting role to play. I found great satisfaction in that work. It gave me the chance to give back and to better serve others—and myself.

This assignment seemed to help breathe new life into me. I began to understand the link between my humanity and my spirituality, especially when I helped develop crime-prevention programs in the schools. It heightened my resolve to work in the best interest of all children and to bring some light into their lives—just as God had done for me. For many years, I tried to explain away the occasional gentle nudges and whispers I continued to receive from an unknown source before I fully understood how they were helping me. It took time for me to acknowledge the presence of the angelic beings who graced not only my life, but the lives of those I served.

CHAPTER 10

TRY TO REMEMBER

As the months passed, I took every opportunity available to obtain instruction about the complex investigations of the crimes against children cases. I attended as many training sessions as my supervisors would permit and devoured books on the subject as well. Over time, I became very proficient and my skills became fine-tuned. My abilities to gauge the innocence or guilt of an alleged perpetrator increased with each new case. I often found that by looking at the iris of a victim's or offender's eyes, I was able to discern an underlying emotion such as sadness, anger, or distrust. It became very easy for me to read their eyes—when I did, I felt like I was connecting directly with their soul. With each question, the chapters of their story unfolded and soon there would be a break in the case or a confession.

With each new case, I couldn't help but shake off an uncomfortable feeling in the back of my mind. I tried to decipher what was bothering me, and realized it was related to the fact that nightmares I had first experienced during childhood had started recurring. On all too many a night, my sleep patterns would be disrupted and I would awake screaming and pouring sweat. The nightmares always followed the same story lines. In one dream, I would be sitting against the headboard of my bed reading a book when all of a sudden a hand would reach out from under the bed and drag me from my peaceful pursuit. In another, I would be dancing on the shoreline of an unknown beach when a shadow would sweep across the sand. The silhouette had no shape to it, but it was dark and able to move quickly. As it loomed closer to me, I'd run into the water and try to hide among the waves. The shadow would always stand by the edge of the water, just waiting for me to walk back onto the beach.

I always felt as if these dreams contained a hidden message and it was trying to emerge from deep in my mind. But try as I might, I was unable to find the key that would unlock the secrets of my mind. That is, until one day in court. As usual, I was on the stand testifying about one of the cases that I had investigated. It was a very trying situation because it involved two pedophiles who had molested their children. The case was further complicated by the fact that the victims were having a tough time testifying against their own parents.

The morning in court started off in a slow-paced manner. I had been testifying for some time on the witness stand. My mind was tired and my patience was wearing thin with the defense attorney's repeated questions. I had worked the midnight shift and had gone straight to court without having had an opportunity to rest or sleep. As the defense attorney fired the next question, I paused to take a breath and to still the anger rising into my throat. When the defense attorney rephrased essentially the same question once again, the prosecutor objected, and the judge requested that both attorneys approach the bench. As I sat and listened to the two lawyers arguing, my mind became a little disoriented. I tried to shake off the confusion, but was unable to do so. The judge suggested a brief adjournment and I was excused temporarily from the witness stand.

When I turned to walk away, my mind became like a kaleidoscope and the floodgates to my memory opened. Recollections of my own childhood came flashing through my mind's eye like a series of video clips, and I saw intermittent events that included me and a man. I immediately recognized the man and realized the events I was suddenly remembering were about my own molestation as a child. As the reels of information gradually became more vivid, I froze in shock. The events were real and I knew the perpetrator's identity. He was someone my parents had trusted. When my mind refocused on the present time, I looked around at the others in the courtroom and was comforted to see that they were all too busy to have noticed my brief departure.

After the judicial recess, my day at the courthouse soon ended. I was relieved not to have to give further testimony. I drove back to my home in a state of utter disbelief. I tried hard to convince myself that the memories were faulty, but try as I might, I could not deny them. So much of my childhood now made sense and the root cause of some of my negative behaviors became apparent: the limited number of childhood memories, the teenage rebellion, the early pregnancy, and of course the nightmares. I had all of the classic symptoms of an abused child. How had I missed them for so long? Did anyone else know? If so, why hadn't they informed me?

Over the next few months, I began to understand my past more fully. With each day, another piece of the puzzle emerged from my memory bank and, before too long, the entire mosaic of my life had been completed. All of the pieces finally fit into place. I understood where I had been and why I had chosen my career path. I had stored the memory of hurt and injury deep inside my psyche. It lay in waiting for the opportune time to be revealed.

But in the revelation of the truth, one more puzzle piece had been located. It was the reason as to why I was so good at investigating the crimes against children cases. I was avenging not only children who had fallen prey to a pedophile, but myself as well. My work helped me resolve all the lingering emotional issues. In convicting offenders, I brought justice to the traumatized children, and to my inner child as well. In a way, through these cases, I had become the guardian angel of these children.

Since that day in the courtroom, I have never had another nightmare about the events of my childhood. There has been no return of the shadows and no hand reaching out from under the bed. My healing came from prosecuting other offenders and from helping each victimized child. I hope that somehow the aid I provided to those child victims will eventually restore some sense of balance for each of them. Because in helping the children, I have also helped myself.

In the spring of 2010, one of these child victims re-entered my life. I was watching one of my eldest granddaughter's volleyball games. As I sat there on the gym's bleachers, I heard a woman's voice say, "Hello, Miss Lillie."

I turned to see a smiling young woman who I immediately recognized standing in front of me. I rose to my feet. She embraced me and introduced me to her husband. I, too, smiled and extended my hand to shake his. As I did so, the young woman said to me, "I wanted my husband to meet the woman who saved me. I've told him all about what you did for me. You helped show me that negative events are not what define me. And you taught me that if I could look past the pain, I could move forward with my life. Well, I took your advice. I went on to finish school and marry this wonderful man. We have two happy and healthy kids. I want you to know it's all because of you saying the words of encouragement I needed to hear. Thank you."

When she finished speaking, I felt tears streaming down my face. I hugged her and said, "I'm so proud of you. May God bless you, your husband, and your children. I'm glad you chose to let the past be the past."

As the two of them walked away hand in hand, I felt such a deep sense of pride—not only for the young woman, but for myself, too. Out of a tattered childhood, she had risen to find a better life. The emotions we both shared seemed to warm the pit of my soul. In my heart, I knew I had lived up to my oath and served as an earthly angel. This encounter once again affirmed for me that one act of kindness can indeed affect the greater good. In reaching out to a little girl long ago, I had helped a young woman of today find her way. By simply uttering a few comforting words in her time of need, I had provided her with the means of moving past her trauma and had encouraged her to flourish. She had found her way and, in turn, would now be able to guide her children to do the same.

I AM WOMAN,
HEAR ME ROAR

As the years passed, I grew more confident in my ability to handle emergency situations. I had worked hard to prove myself and had honed my police skills. In my mind, I had finally achieved a balance and felt somewhat comfortable in my profession. And it gave me such a sense of pride to know I had acquired a fine reputation—especially as a woman officer serving in the field. The fellowship of several of my colleagues provided support that helped me to prosper, but I often felt isolated. Those feelings began to dissipate when I met Ron, an officer from a neighboring police department. We seemed to bond instantly and we quickly established a rare form of friendship, not a romantic connection, but a strong sense of unconditional love and camaraderie.

One day as I was patrolling the city, I received a call from a dispatcher requesting assistance in a bordering community concerning a domestic situation. I arrived at the scene within minutes. In approaching the house, I observed a tall and heavyset woman standing at the front door. Her face was covered in blood and her eyes were swollen from crying. Her white T-shirt was soaked in blood, as was her short blond hair. She held a dish towel up to her face, and I could see that the terry cloth fabric was also stained crimson. I approached her front door and said, "Are you alright? I received an emergency dispatch regarding a domestic situation. Did you call the police? May I come in?"

The woman nodded her head and politely led me into her home. The living room furniture was in disarray and there were pools of blood on the floor. This preliminary evidence clearly suggested that a struggle had ensued and that she had been assaulted.

Her tears began to flow as we walked to her kitchen. We sat for a few minutes while she regained her composure. During my initial moments of interviewing her, she was not forthcoming about who had committed the assault. Eventually I began to ask her more direct, pertinent questions: who, what, when, where, and why. She responded in soft tones and muted sobs, and she finally identified her husband as her assailant.

For a few brief moments she defended her husband, and even ended her statement by saying she loved him. It was almost as if she had forgotten about what had just happened, and had transcended to another place and time. I sat for a couple moments and listened as she reminisced, and watched her hardened features soften as she recalled fond memories of the man she had married. For a moment I, too, cast my mind back to the time in my life when the soft words of a loving husband had been a part of my daily existence. In doing so I felt a greater sense of empathy for this woman. When she finished talking, I calmly reminded her of the current situation and asked if she was willing to press charges against her husband. Reluctantly, she nodded her head and whispered a quiet, "Yes."

With the interview complete, I explained that another police officer would follow up with her about filing a restraining order and a formal complaint. I asked if she desired to receive any medical attention and she declined. She thanked me for my kindness and walked me to the front door.

When I emerged onto the porch, a man came around the corner of the house. He briskly walked up the steps; in a flash, he was standing next to me. I knew instinctively that he must be the woman's husband. No words were necessary. His manner and her reaction to his presence said it all. Within seconds, he began screaming obscenities. He was furious at her for calling the police.

"Leave the premises or I will arrest you!" I shouted.

Without any warning, the man lunged at me and yelled, "Yeah, you and what army?"

Before I had time to gather my thoughts, I grabbed him and shoved him over the front porch rail. He landed face-down on the ground. I ran down and managed to cuff him with one swift sweep of the hand. As I lifted him from the ground, a patrol car pulled up along the curb and an officer I did not recognize asked me, "Are you okay? Where is your backup?"

"I don't have any," I responded.

The officer just smiled, shook his head, and said, "I heard about you. The guys in your department said you were tough. I guess they were right."

He stepped out of the patrol car and helped me place the man into its backseat. As we were doing this, I noticed some men sitting outside a mill across the street. It appeared they had been eating their lunches. All at once, they began to clap and started singing "I am woman, hear me roar."

The men began to laugh out loud as they sang and clapped. Their laughter was contagious and soon the officer and I found ourselves laughing, too. He extended his hand and introduced himself as Ron. He explained that now that he had witnessed my abilities for himself he, too, would be able to sing my accolades. I thanked him and welcomed him as well. As we parted ways, I knew I had made a new friend. In the following years, our friendship grew, as did our mutual respect for each other.

Over the next 24 years, Ron and I shared a deep bond. In good times, we celebrated. In bad times, we supported each other. And in the truly ugly times, we shed tears and held each other's hands. We also shared a passion for writing, and during many a slow evening shift, we talked about our creative work.

One late afternoon in March of 2012, I learned that Ron had died unexpectedly. In the course of mowing his parents' lawn, his big heart beat for the last time. For a brief moment, my heart stopped beating as well. The friendship we had had been severed and life suddenly felt somehow incomplete.

My heart and mind fell to pieces when I thought about not ever seeing that big lug again. But the night after he died, a miracle occurred: Ron's spirit appeared to me. I felt blessed by his presence. He showed me a visualization of what had transpired on the lawn on that fateful day. I saw Ron's spirit rise and leave his body, and for a moment he lingered above it. He appeared to be confused about what had happened, but said not a word.

In the days that followed, he made several more visits. On his second manifestation, he just stood there, again saying nothing to me. The third time, he finally spoke. He asked a question in that familiar voice that was uniquely his: "What the hell happened?"

I smiled and tried to explain the circumstances that had brought about his passing.

"But I wasn't ready," he replied.

I didn't know what to say, so I did my best to soothe his troubled spirit and to help ease him through his transition to another domain.

On Ron's fourth appearance, he whispered a message for his wife. I held those words sacred and dutifully delivered the message as asked.

On the fifth occasion, I saw Ron standing at the cemetery, watching his own memorial service. He had no words for me that day. He just stood there smiling, taking in everything. He seemed grateful for the send-off from his family, friends, and colleagues. And when the mayor placed Ron's police jacket on his daughter's shoulders, I saw a tear fall from the deceased chief's eye. It was not a tear of sadness, but one of pride.

In that moment, I experienced another vision. It was of his daughter's future and her days yet to be. What I saw was her all grown up and wearing a police uniform.

In the days that followed his burial, Ron manifested himself to me twice more. Again he said nothing, but merely smiled that all-knowing smile he had so often worn. With each visit from my beloved friend, my anger at his unexpected passing seemed to dissipate and a new-found peace took hold, for I knew he was now in a better place.

Ron's death also taught me a valuable lesson. Because of it, I came to understand the importance of not waiting to pursue my dreams. One of our final conversations had been all about that very subject. Ron had told me how proud he was of me for writing and publishing my first book. He was pleased I had risen above my setbacks and had achieved a comeback of my own making. On that afternoon, he had given me a hug and a mischievous smile had crossed his face. I had hugged him back and said, "I love you."

He just shook his head and said, "I don't know why."

As he walked away from me then, I of course didn't know that it was the last time I would see him alive. If I had, I would have hugged him just a little tighter and held him to this earth with all the strength that I could muster.

When Ron died, my tears fell in unison with so many other individuals', but I found I was unable to articulate verbally what Ron's friendship had truly come to mean. So as usual, I took up the pen. As I began to write, the words flowed easily from my hand to the paper's surface. And before too long, I realized the words I was writing were those Ron's spirit had shared with me—a link between my earthly plain and his heavenly domain.

CHAPTER 12

THE RHYTHM
OF TWO HEARTS

As my daughter grew into her teenage years, we struggled with the emotional ups and downs of adolescence. Having a mother who also happened to be a cop made things a bit more difficult for Vanessa. Most teenagers view obtaining a driver's license as a rite of passage, but since I had responded to all too many vehicle accidents caused by teenage recklessness, I faced a real dilemma in deciding whether or not Vanessa was ready for such a responsibility. When the time came for her to take driving lessons, I was nervous. The incidents I had seen usually related to some young person taking a risk by driving too fast, listening to loud music, or just not paying attention to the road. As a mother and a police officer, I felt double the anxiety. Although Vanessa was 17, I still somehow saw her as my little girl. The thought of her out on the road, facing all types of precarious situations, made me hesitate in giving her my approval. However, after several very lengthy discussions, we came to the conclusion that it was indeed time for her to become a licensed driver. With my increasing workload and ever-changing duties at the police department, her driving would make life much easier for us both. I pushed aside my misgivings, gave in to her request, and off she went to the races.

A few weeks after Vanessa received her driver's license, she asked to take my car to visit a friend. It would be her first time driving alone. Prior to that, I had not allowed her to use my car unless I was with her. My intuition told me not to let her go, but I gave in. As she pulled out of the driveway, I had a strong sense of foreboding. I didn't quite understand what I was sensing, but I could also not shake it off.

About an hour after Vanessa left the house, I decided to take a shower. I went through my normal routine of lathering up my hair. As I was scrubbing my head, I heard a voice yell, "Mommy!"

I stopped for a moment and listened more intently. Perhaps Vanessa had arrived back home and was calling out to let me know? As I continued to enjoy the warmth of the water, I heard another voice whisper: "Your daughter had an accident."

My mind raced, and I became very distraught at the thought that Vanessa could be hurt somewhere and without me. I hurried to finish my shower and began making telephone calls to her friends. This was before cell phones were in common use, so it wasn't easy to track people down. I paced around the house, waiting for someone to call. When the telephone finally rang, it was a police officer on the other end of the line. He was calling to let me know that Vanessa had been in a traffic accident. No one had been injured, but Vanessa was upset. He said he would be bringing Vanessa home, accompanied by the other parties involved.

When they arrived, I was embarrassed by my appearance. I hadn't had time to dress, so there I stood at my front door in a pink terry cloth robe, brown furry slippers with a large moose head at the end of each toe, and a towel tightly wrapped around my wet head. When they entered the room, I felt myself blush. Vanessa just shook her head and the police officer, who was a colleague, started to laugh out loud. For a moment, I just stood there looking at him but then I started laughing myself. The humor helped to break the tension. Before too long, all was resolved and the small entourage left my home.

It wasn't until later that evening, when Vanessa and I were eating dinner, that I asked her if she remembered the accident. She did, and mentioned that when she struck the other car she had yelled for me. She said she had screamed the word "Mommy."

I looked at her and said, "I knew you had called to me to help. I heard a voice yell the exact same word while I was taking a shower. And then I heard the words, 'Your daughter had an accident.'"

Vanessa looked amazed at what I said. She then nodded her head in apparent understanding. I shrugged my shoulders and said, "You know I have a sixth sense when it comes to those I love. Most especially you and my dad."

She just smiled and we quietly finished our dinner. Later that night as I lay in bed, I thought about the voice that had warned me about the accident. It had been the same voice I had heard so often before. However, this was the first time I had ever heard *Vanessa's* voice send me a message. Although I was grateful for the ability to be so connected to her, I wondered how it had come to pass. It was as if our two hearts were beating in synchronicity, and our minds and souls were intertwined as one as well. In that moment of reflection, I recalled the words of the Greek philosopher Plato, who said that human beings were only a part of a soul, only half of a whole. Plato believed that at birth the soul split apart and separated. The two halves then spent the rest of eternity searching for the other half of their being. The souls keep wandering until such time that they find one another and regain their sense of wholeness again. So, perhaps, it was with Vanessa and me. She is not my soul mate in the traditional sense of Plato's meaning, but our souls are linked in a familial way nonetheless. We are travelers, pilgrims who chose to walk together and aid each other on our journeys.

What I came to realize from this event was integral in reinforcing my beliefs about a mother's love. No other bond is as strong as that of a mother and her child. It is primal, and is imperative to the child's existence and survival in this universe. In that moment when I heard my child's voice calling for me, I had that revelation, and the definition of maternal love came full circle in my mind and was forever etched on my heart.

CHAPTER 13

NOTES FROM A SQUAD ROOM

As is true for many of the life lessons I have learned, I usually attained the knowledge the hard way. Not because I refused to be instructed in the way of the world but simply because I have always had a tough time accepting the inhumanity of humanity.

While on patrol one day, I received a call from a dispatcher with an urgent message for me to contact Dad. I drove straight to the house. When I arrived, I noticed Dad was sitting on the front porch. He had a letter in his hand and was intently reading it. As I walked the short distance from the car to the porch, I could see that he was distressed. Normally when I arrived he would jump to his feet, smile, and kiss my cheek. But on this particular day, he barely looked up at me. From the expression on his face, it was obvious that whatever he was reading had caused him great pain. Before I could ask any questions, Dad gestured for me to sit down next to him on the glider. I obliged. Without saying a word, he handed the letter to me.

As I read the text, I felt my anger flare. Although the letter was short in its narrative, the content of the message was filled with pure hate. It contained many racial slurs and terrible comments about Vanessa and her choices in men. It was also very threatening in its tone.

When I finished reading, I paused before I looked up at Dad. I needed a few minutes to wrap my mind around the content and the author's possible motives for writing it. My adrenaline surged and my heart raced. How was I to respond to this? On top of everything, it was anonymous. What a coward! I felt unable to defend my family against an unknown enemy.

Before I could even speak, Dad asked, "What do you intend to do about this situation?"

I looked at him in surprise. From his tone, it was obvious the letter had done its job. Dad appeared to be having a hard time remaining calm. We spent a few minutes in silence before either of us spoke again. By that point, Dad was seething and looked as if he was about to explode. So as a means of balancing both of our emotions, I spoke with as much self-control as possible.

"How do you expect me to respond to this?" I asked.

"There is only one way. You have to take control of the situation, and of Vanessa as well. She has to stop dating this young man and start worrying about her reputation and our family's as well," Dad said.

On hearing his comment, I felt my heart heave in complete disappointment. The emotion of the moment almost made me utter words I knew I would regret. As I looked into Dad's eyes, I could see his pain. Although I knew him to be a good man, I did not agree with him about this situation. On that day, his heart was not in the right place, nor was he behaving like his usual tolerant self.

As I regained my senses, I could feel the maternal instinct in me begin to rise. But before I could respond, Dad shared his thoughts about interracial dating and the impact it might have on Vanessa's life. From all he shared, it was apparent his mind was made up.

"I need time to digest this and consider the ramifications. You can't expect me to know how to immediately handle a situation that tears at my very heartstrings," I finally replied.

I then got up off the glider and kissed him on top of his head. I felt a lump of emotion building inside my throat. It was hard to swallow back all of the feelings now surging. Especially the deep sense of sadness and loss—it was obvious my relationship with Dad had instantaneously changed. For the first time since my pregnancy, I felt the sting of his disapproval. And it was also obvious to me that our roles in the family had suddenly been reversed. For the first time in my life, I felt a deep disappointment in my father's behavior.

That day, I left the porch knowing that our bond had been strained. I walked to the patrol car fighting back tears. As I opened the car door, I looked up at Dad one last time. He was still standing on the porch, and he made a half-hearted attempt to wave good-bye. In that moment, I realized that my life as I knew it had been altered. I couldn't quite put my finger on why, but I heard the voice inside my ears sending me a warning message: Vanessa's relationship would become the catalyst for a civil war of sorts. It didn't take very long for the rest of the family to hear about the letter and to realize that I sided with my daughter. Although I was apprehensive at first, I decided to stand by her and respect her decision. After all, it was the appropriate thing to do. I had raised my daughter to believe all of God's children were the same and that race, gender, and religion were not relevant to loving or being loved.

Over the next few months, Dad and I both received a plethora of hate mail and harassing telephone calls. For several months after that, my daughter and I argued with so-called friends and family members who disapproved of interracial coupling. And I battled with my fellow police officers in the squad room about it as well—some of the letters had even been sent to the station. Eventually, after much contemplation, I chose to leave the force and to accept a position as the chief law enforcement officer with a college security department. In retrospect, it was an excellent choice for both Vanessa's and my well-being.

That decision to move on seemed to ease some tension. By entering an academic environment, which had a comparatively global outlook, and leaving the small-town mind-set behind, I found a whole new world waiting to be discovered. In time, Vanessa and I found some peace in our lives. She retreated to the safety of her boyfriend's family. I embraced my new job. On the campus, I found new friends, and we were truly blessed by having some people around us who stepped forward to help us through that ordeal. Although my trust in human nature had begun to fade, it was restored by the wonderful friends who arrived to enrich our lives.

CHAPTER 14

AT HEAVEN'S GATE

Shortly before Vanessa entered college, we moved back into my parents' home. On a police officer's salary, I couldn't help fund her higher education and maintain our townhouse as well. It also happened that, shortly before we relocated, Dad was diagnosed with liver cancer. So the move would benefit not only us, but would help Dad in his time of need.

Vanessa was still very much involved with the same boyfriend, and the family's position on him had not changed. Vanessa tried to maintain a low profile, but her relationship was still a hot topic. To further complicate the matter, her boyfriend had begun using drugs. This only worsened the family's opinion of him. Meanwhile, Dad was in the middle of receiving cancer treatments and the strong doses of cytotoxic drugs altered his personality and demeanor. The once levelheaded man I had known morphed into a being that I did not recognize.

As the early summer season arrived and the temperature outside heated up, the temperaments of family members intensified inside the house, too. There were near-constant arguments about Dad's treatments and Vanessa's love life. One particular evening, I arrived home late from work and walked in on Vanessa and Dad arguing.

As I listened to Vanessa try to defend herself and her relationship, I could hear Dad's voice getting louder. Each new word escalated the level of anger between the two of them; I had never witnessed such a heated debate between them before. My heart ached to watch the two most important people in my life battling. I tried to intervene, but when I attempted to do so, Dad started using very offensive language. Vanessa and I froze. As we stood there in shock, I replied, "How dare you speak to her like that! Where is all of this hate coming from?"

It was Vanessa who spoke next. She looked straight into Dad's eyes and said, "If this is how you feel, then there is only one thing to do. I'll move out and find my own apartment."

As she finished speaking, she began to cry and ran from the room. When Vanessa fled past me, I tried to take hold of her arm and soothe her, but she pulled away from me and in an instant she was gone.

I turned back to look at Dad when I heard him yell, "Go, then! Nobody wants you here anymore."

Even though that moment remains surreally long in my memory, I recall it took but a second for me to regain my composure and respond to his insensitive rant.

"Dad, she *is* wanted here. I want Vanessa in my life. As long as she is here, I can protect her. You shouldn't have talked to her that way. She is a good girl. But it is obvious you're not the man that I thought you were. Do me a favor: when you find my dad, will you please tell him that I miss him and would like him to come home?"

I left Dad standing there and ran from the house, hoping to catch up with Vanessa. But she was already gone and so was her car. Despite my repeated attempts to contact her, I didn't manage to speak to her again that night. When Vanessa returned home the next morning, she was still quite distressed and did not want to discuss the previous night's events. She indicated she was tired and just wanted to sleep. Over the next few days, Vanessa behaved in a very sullen manner. Each time I tried to broach the subject of the argument, she refused to discuss it with me.

A few days later, Vanessa told me that she had found an apartment and was moving in with her boyfriend. I was devastated. Although I had been supportive of the relationship in the past, I was worried. Vanessa had never lived away from home, much less with a man who was exhibiting questionable behavior. The more we talked about it, however, the more I realized she had made up her mind. After all, she was now an adult and old enough to make her own decisions and to act on them as well.

Within a week's time, our lives were turned upside down. Vanessa packed her belongings onto a truck one night, and my heart ached as she pulled away from the house. When she gave her last wave and yelled good-bye, the tears welling in my eyes formed into full drops. Somehow, in that moment, I had a tough time perceiving her as a grown woman. My thoughts took me back to a place in time when she was just a little child clinging to her mama for support. I remembered her first day of kindergarten as a tiny, blond-haired, blue-eyed girl and my heart heaved at the memory.

As my mind returned to the present, I wondered just how long I would have to wait before my little girl came back. When I turned to walk toward my apartment in the house, I realized that Dad was still standing there. I decided it would be best just to go inside and not confront him.

However, without missing a beat, Dad said, "Well, she's finally gone. Now maybe we can have some peace around here again."

On hearing his unkind words, I replied, "Dad, I want you to know I, too, intend on moving out. Your behavior was unacceptable. If it wasn't for what you said, Vanessa would still be living here. If something happens to her, I'll never forgive you. She is a wonderful young woman and I'm very proud of her. Your actions do not reflect the teachings of the Bible, nor do you resemble the man who raised me to believe all men were created equal. So do us all a favor. When you leave this earth and meet Saint Peter in Heaven, ask him who was right: you or Vanessa. And when it is Vanessa's time, please greet her at the gate and apologize. Now leave me alone, and I'll do the same for you."

Dad attempted to respond to my comments, but in the familiar gesture he always used with his children, I raised my hand in the air and he fell silent. Over the next few days, I agonized over the thought of my daughter setting up house away from me. Until that time, she and I had not been away from each other for more than a few weeks' time. The apartment seemed so empty without her. My heart ached for the once-harmonious relationship we had shared. It felt like all of the pieces of my intricate family puzzle had become separated. How could this situation ever be resolved? All three of us had similarly stubborn personalities. When challenged, we would stand our proverbial ground.

Shortly after Vanessa moved out, it was my birthday. I was in no mood for any sort of celebration, but as usual, I came home from work to find a birthday cake and card waiting for me. Apparently, Dad had made his way upstairs to my apartment and placed them on my bed. However, this year I had no desire to read the card and I had no appetite for the taste of the cake either. Within minutes of my arrival, my telephone rang. Dad was on the other end. He shared that he was hungry for some cake.

"I'm not interested in celebrating my birthday—or in eating any cake with you," I said.

Dad quickly replied, "I'm sorry for what happened."

I could hear the emotion in his voice and I almost weakened my stance. But my hurt feelings prevailed.

"You don't owe me the apology—you owe it to Vanessa. If she is willing to forgive you, then so am I."

Before Dad could respond, I hung up the receiver. That was a tough position for me to take just then. I knew he might succumb to the cancer at any time. That might have been my last opportunity to hear him sing "Happy Birthday" as only he could sing it.

A few hours later, the telephone rang again. I answered. It was Vanessa. She extended her birthday wishes and asked me to come downstairs.

Vanessa explained that she and Dad had had a long discussion. She accepted his apology and felt it was time for all of us to forgive and forget.

As I listened to her words, I was once again amazed by my loving daughter. For someone so young, she was already so wise. I marveled at her ability to see things in such an objective manner. I came to discover it wouldn't be the last life lesson I learned from Vanessa.

CHAPTER 15

THE SAFE
PASSAGE OF A FATHER
AND A SON

My earliest recollections of Dad reinforce my feeling that we were more than biologically related—we were spiritually entwined as well. It seemed as if our hearts shared the same rhythm and ran in the same direction, much as the waters of a river moving in unison from the same source. I firmly believe that my father's and my heart beat as one. He was the nucleus of our family's life and an oak tree to all. I felt if he died, a part of my spirit would leave this earth. As a child, I remember often praying that God would permit me to die before Dad, because I could not fathom a life without his presence. And despite our recent disagreements, I still felt a very deep connection to him.

Being so interconnected allowed for me to hear whispers and guidance about Dad from the angels on many occasions. Before Dad was diagnosed with liver cancer, I heard words that made my heart ache. I was with Dad at his home, and we were sitting out on the porch, enjoying the sunshine and just chatting. He was trying to tell one of his jokes. Dad had a habit of not being able to finish his own punch lines without bursting into laughter. As he sat there amused at himself, I heard a whisper in my ear: "He is sick. His blood is not healthy."

On hearing those words, I froze with fear. How could it be true? Dad was a strong and healthy man, and he looked wonderfully fit. I tried to ease the feelings of dread that instantly arose and willed myself to relax.

Then the voice spoke again. I listened as it shared the following words: "He will only live for another few years." The words of foreboding paralyzed my ability to even think straight. How was it possible Dad would be gone so soon? He had always professed he would live to the ripe old age of 123, and he was a long way off from achieving that goal; he had barely entered into his late sixties.

During his initial surgery, some complications arose. He suffered extensive bleeding and his physicians were concerned about his survival. They explained to us as we sat in the waiting room that he was still unconscious, and that the next few hours would be crucial in determining whether or not he would recover. After a time, I again heard a familiar voice whisper in my ear, "He is awake."

As these words echoed through the recesses of my mind, I saw a vision of dad's mother, Situ, enter the room. When I looked at her, her spirit smiled. I instantly knew that she had come to check on her son's well-being. She stood over her family members, all the while smiling at her loved ones. I could see the very essence of her being, and it was radiant and surrounded in a white light. I could smell the fragrance of roses, too. My grandmother had so loved her garden. She had grown beautiful rosebushes in her yard and taken great care of them. She had tended to the many blossoms just as she had watched over her children. Dad and his mom had a very special relationship, and somehow their bond appeared to have now transcended time and space. I only hoped my grandmother had not arrived with the intention of taking Dad with her to the boundaries of Heaven's gate.

On seeing her spirit, I turned to my mother and said, "Dad's awake, and Situ is here."

Mom turned toward me rather flippantly and replied, "Don't give me any of that witchy-poo stuff today. He's not awake. The nurse would have notified us."

Just as she uttered those very words, the nurse entered the waiting room. She explained that Dad had finally opened his eyes. I looked at Mom and smiled. The nurse then shared that Dad was asking to see Mom. She added that only two people would be allowed to see him at a time. Mom asked me to join her.

When we arrived at Dad's bedside, it was easy to see that his body was in great distress. He was connected to several machines, his breathing was labored, and his vital signs were weak. The constant beeping of the devices only heightened our anxiety. Neither of us were prepared to witness him in such a frail state. Our once-vibrant patriarch looked so tired and worn. It took every bit of my strength not to cry out.

As Mom bent down to kiss his forehead, Dad opened his eyes. In them, I could see how much he was suffering. And yet he mustered up enough strength to smile. His eyes twinkled. Mom began to weep. For that moment, Dad ceased to be a patient. He became her husband again, and soothed her with his words. As I watched the silent dance of magic between them, it affirmed what a strong love they shared. It was such a poignant moment. For a few minutes, it seemed that all was frozen in time and I was observing a transfer of love between two individuals, who just happened to be my parents. It seemed that they had a mystical, invisible cord that connected their hearts. I was moved at witnessing a glimpse of the connection that linked Mom and Dad not only as husband and wife, but spirit to spirit. And in the stillness of that hospital room, another "aha" moment occurred. I had been privileged to observe two hearts merging as one, two spirits finding their other half. And in that moment of revelation, I finally understood the theory of spiritual oneness.

When it was my turn, I bent down to give him a kiss. When I did, he removed the oxygen mask from his face and smiled. In a very hoarse voice he whispered, "Tell me why a woman who can wrap her heart around a thousand people can't find one man to love?"

In between my tears, I began to laugh. "Well, Dad, if you are waiting for me to remarry, you might have to hang around for quite a while."

Dad tried to laugh at my retort, but was unable to and merely shut his eyes. I left his hospital room that night praying to God for a miracle. Although his awakening from the surgical procedure that day had been a blessing, a full cure would never come.

It was impossible to picture a life without Dad. After his first surgery, the schedule of caring for him became hectic and the stress level in the household escalated. My mom, my siblings, Vanessa, and I shared the responsibility of spending time with Dad and attending to his health-care needs. Each of us took turns driving him to his doctor's appointments and the hospital for his treatments. As Dad's health deteriorated, though, so did his perspective on life. His usual positive demeanor delved sometimes into dark moods that I had not observed in him before. The strong-spirited and muscular man of my youth had begun to change into someone I barely recognized. Gone were the bright sparkle of his lovely green eyes and the belly laugh we had so often heard. He lost the desire to engage in outside activities, and when he did, it was clear that he had lost the quickness in his step. It was obvious his body was growing frailer by the day and his spirit was preparing for its voyage home. From the messages I continued to hear, I knew it would be only a matter of time before Dad would journey to the heavens above.

On September 10, 1994, Dad succumbed to his illness. For over two years, he had put up a valiant fight trying to rid his body of that dreaded disease. Each treatment humbled his once-strong body and brilliant psyche. It was time to say good-bye to the head of our family and a man beloved by all who knew him. As he took his final breaths my mother, younger sister, Vanessa, her boyfriend, and I stood watch over him. Each of us wanted to be with him in his last moments of life. As his breathing became labored, I again smelled that same scent of roses I had on the day of his first surgery. I looked up to the area above my dad's head. There stood Situ once more. She was smiling at her son and gently caressing his brow. In Dad's moment of great need, his mother had reached out from the afterlife to gently guide him safely home. I then saw the vision of an angel. He was standing to Situ's left shoulder. Both of their beings were beautifully enshrouded by white light. As Dad took his last breaths, I witnessed what I believe to be his soul leaving his body. I saw a burst of pure, white light emanate from his chest. As Dad made one last exhale, he smiled. A light shined down upon him and encompassed his entire being. When I looked at the vital signs monitor, I noticed Dad had taken his last breath exactly one hour and twenty-three minutes after the ventilator had been removed.

It was in that moment that I truly understood the term of "the white light of grace." Despite Dad's illness and the pain that had constantly riddled his body, he had never lost his faith or his belief that God would provide him with the grace to endure. And in that moment of his spiritual rapture, I knew Dad was being carried to his celestial home.

During Dad's memorial, we discovered the true impact he had had on the lives of others, and most especially on children. During the viewing, generations of former students took the time to share stories about Dad. As we listened, chapters of his life we hadn't known about began to unfold. One by one, stories of how he mentored a student, provided lunch money, or donated a coat or a pair of shoes were shared. At one point Mom turned to us and said, "Now I know where all of Dad's money went. He spent it on his other kids!"

When Dad was laid to rest, there were so many people in attendance. As a bugle played taps and a 21-gun salute finished, many tears were shed. I left the cemetery feeling heartsick and wondering how life could continue without Dad's presence. Later that night, as I lay in bed, I once again felt the presence of the Blue Man. As in times past, his angelic love and light comforted me. The beloved Archangel had manifested to ease my pain. Although he spoke no words, I felt solace in his fellowship.

CHAPTER 16

IGNITE MY
HEART LIGHT

When Dad died, a huge part of my heart went with him into his grave. His death had such a terrible impact on the entire family, too. We all felt lost without his guidance. He was one of those men who everybody felt comfortable turning to in a time of need. I remember feeling so angry with God. On the morning that he passed, I went to my car and screamed at the Lord.

"Why? How can you take such a good man when there are so many evil men still walking the earth?"

In that moment, I questioned my faith. I felt that my connection to God had been severed. In the following months, I turned away from my religious beliefs. After I attended Dad's funeral service, I quit going to church.

As the days passed and our family moved through the process of grieving for Dad, we revisited many moments from his life. Each of us found it beneficial to share our favorite stories about him. As I reminisced alongside the others, though, I had a tough time shaking off the remorse I felt. Although my regrets were few, they tore at my heart-strings. My deepest regrets had to do with my teenage pregnancy and failed marriage. Whenever I would sit in quiet reflection, my mind would twist and turn as a cascade of melodramas replayed inside my mind. The most significant of them was the night I had told my parents about the unintended pregnancy.

On that quiet May evening of long ago, the sanctity of our family life had been immediately changed. My boyfriend, a beloved aunt, and I broke the news to Dad first, and I could see the hurt in his eyes. Yet instead of responding in anger, he looked extremely sad. The look on his face did more damage to my psyche than any unkind words he might have spewed. I felt instantaneous shame.

I recall Dad saying, "I'm disappointed in your behavior. But no matter the circumstance, a child is a blessing from God. We'll find a way to work this out."

Dad turned to my then-boyfriend and asked him about his intentions toward the baby and me. He indicated he wanted to marry me and raise our child.

"Then you better start calling me Dad," he had replied. "But know that if you ever hurt her, I will kill you."

I clearly remember Dad giving me a half-smile. He then quietly mumbled he was going to tell Situ the news and it would be up to us to tell my mom. As he walked away, though, I noticed that his shoulders and head were hunched. I thought I could hear him sob. It was one of the moments in life that rips at the very fiber of your being.

Mom's reaction was more like the one I had anticipated. Unlike Dad, who responded with great compassion, Mom was furious. She said words that were very damaging to me and cut at the very core of our relationship. It would take many years before I found the ability to forgive her—and myself as well.

The night before my wedding day, I came home to find my dad sitting on his bed and holding my three younger sisters in his arms. He was crying—a behavior that was not common practice for Dad. I asked him if there was a problem. At my question, he raised his hand in the air—a gesture that we all knew meant "silence."

Dad looked straight at me. "You were the smart one. You were supposed to be a doctor or a lawyer. But tomorrow, you're going to be nothing but somebody's damn wife."

Before I could react to his words, he added, "Leave me alone. I have nothing left to say to you tonight."

I ran from the room, sobbing. I knew I had hurt him with my actions, but until that moment, I had not realized the depth of his emotional pain. I spent the night feeling sick to my stomach and unable to sleep. When I went downstairs in the morning, I found Dad at his usual place in the kitchen, preparing breakfast for everyone. He greeted me with a smile, in the same manner that he always had. We didn't speak about the events of the night before, and we would not talk of them again for many years to come.

Later that day, when he was about to walk me down the aisle, we stopped as we entered the back of the church. He gave me a hug. In my ear he whispered, "Are you sure you want to go through with this? You don't have to if you don't want to. If you choose to walk out this church door, I'll make things right with your mother."

In that moment of confusion and fear, his words made me want to scream, *"No! I don't want to get married. I just want to keep my baby!"*

But how could I refuse to go through with the marriage? I was raised to believe that pregnancy outside of marriage was a sin. Since my condition had already caused so much embarrassment and pain for our family, I didn't feel like I could subject my parents to any further humiliation.

With a halfhearted smile on my face, I replied, "There is only one way out of this mess, and it is down that aisle."

With tears now streaming down both of our faces, we walked down the aisle together, trying to smile and pretend that we were both glad about the wedding, that the tears were those of joy. Ironically, this poignant moment between Dad and me was captured in a photograph that is a part of my wedding album.

It wasn't until the weeks preceding my dad's death that he and I again spoke of that long ago night before my wedding or the hurtful words that he had uttered. I had the opportunity to visit him in his hospital room on a daily basis because the college where I was then working was in close proximity. On one particular day, I arrived while Dad's physician was in the room. I couldn't quite help but notice that the doctor was avoiding any direct questions that related to Dad's illness or future prognosis. My intuition kicked into high gear. I began to suspect the doctor was being less than candid, so when he walked out of the room, I followed him. I asked him to explain the new complications to Dad's condition. At first he hesitated, but then the doctor explained that he expected Dad to live only a few more months. The cancer had returned and metastasized in other areas of his body.

When I heard his words, my heart wrenched and my stomach turned. I felt like someone had driven a hot poker into my chest. I could not catch my breath, and I felt the hallway begin to spin. I reached out to brace myself against a wall and tried to regain some composure and restraint.

With some effort, I pulled myself together, wiped the tears from my face, and returned to Dad's hospital room.

As I reentered, I noticed another patient lying in the bed across the room. The man was surrounded by others who I assumed were members of his family. Dad introduced us and, although I was not in much of a mood to be cordial, I smiled.

The man then said, "So you're Lillie. I've heard so much about you. Your dad has been telling us how beautiful you are."

I turned to Dad and questioned, "I'm beautiful?"

"Well of course you are, girl," Dad replied.

The man politely continued, "Your dad has been telling us how smart you are, too."

Turning toward Dad again, I retorted, "I'm smart?"

Dad responded, "Well of course you are, girl."

His roommate then added one last comment that I felt in my very core. "And your dad has told us how proud he is of you."

I was unable to respond for a moment, so I quickly turned in Dad's direction. As the tears poured from my eyes, I looked straight at him and said, "You're proud of me?"

"Well of course I am, girl. How many dads get to boast that their daughter is a chief of police?"

With Dad's last comment, my mind whirled back to that moment in time some twenty years prior when he had told me how disappointed he was in me. I regressed and became the same young woman who knew she had brought emotional suffering to those she loved—resulting in so much damage to my own self-esteem. I ran to my dad's bed, laid my head on his stomach, and sobbed. I began to recount that painful day. As I did, Dad started laughing out loud.

When I lifted my head up, I saw a familiar smile on his face. He rubbed the top of my head and said, "I guess you're not as smart as I thought you were, girl. When I spoke those words all those years ago, it wasn't to hurt you. It was to motivate you. I knew that you of all my children needed to be challenged in order to succeed. So that night, I lit a flame to challenge you to set some future goals. And it now seems that I ignited a rocket that has soared."

As he finished speaking, I had a profound realization. On that night so many years ago, when my life was in a tailspin, Dad knew what he needed to say to me in order to help me achieve a more promising future.

I left his hospital room that day with bittersweet emotions. It was fortunate that he and I had the opportunity to talk about that painful memory. The reality of his impending death made me realize, though, that there would not be enough time left to say all of the things we needed to say.

When Dad left this world, he did so knowing he was loved by his wayward daughter, and I knew he loved me. It was the first time I realized the importance of making peace and asking for forgiveness while both individuals have the chance to apologize to one another. It would also be the first step in my awakening to the significance of forgiveness. That defining moment helped Dad and me find our own paths to redemption, and also highlighted for me that there were others I still needed to forgive, including my mother. But for a while, I allowed myself permission just to mourn. In time, I would reach out to Mom and try to find a means for healing both our wounded hearts.

In the darkest moments of my life, I have felt Dad's presence. I always know when he is near because my sense of smell is permeated with the aroma of coffee—a very distinct and unmistakable scent. I've associated him with the smell of coffee since my early childhood. The first thing Dad did when he would awake each morning was make a pot of coffee. He would then pour a cup full of the brown fluid and hand it to my mother. In my early years of policing, I would at times stop home during midnight shifts. And on those nights when he knew I was on patrol, Dad would often be waiting in the kitchen, brewing some java for me. To this day, the aroma of coffee instantly prompts thoughts of him. At times, I have smelled it in the remotest of locations. Once, when I was traveling at night through the mountains of West Virginia, I became a bit fearful because I thought I might be lost. All at once, I smelled coffee in the car. And I immediately knew it was a sign from dear old Dad telling me that all was well. I truly believe Dad was in the car with me, and that he guided me in the right direction, just as he had done so many times in the past.

CHAPTER 17

A MOTHER'S LOVE

Like many mother-daughter relationships, mine is complex. It is intertwined with regrets and a great deal of misunderstanding, especially in the early years of my life, when she and I appeared unable to achieve any synchronicity or balance. Sometimes when my mother was asked about our relationship, she would reply, "Lillie came out of the womb telling me to go to hell and kissing her dad. The sun rose and set on her father. I could do nothing right and he could do no wrong."

Medical research implies that the touch or scent of a mother is usually the first sensation a newborn baby will register. With a limited ability to see, these impressions bond the child to the mother. This bond is the link that, in turn, provides the little one with a sense of security and that allows him or her to grow and feel that he or she is safe. When this bond is underdeveloped or broken, the child often feels abandoned and lost. And so it seemed this is what happened with my mother and me. With so many siblings, there never seemed to be any time for the two of us to connect in a meaningful way. Being one of the eldest, I felt obligated to help with the younger children. Mom's eventual return to college only heightened my sense of insecurity. As a result, I felt unprepared to participate in a world that seemed less than secure. And when I became pregnant, the breach between Mom and me became even deeper.

For many months after Dad's death, I continued to feel a great sense of loss. Without his constant presence, life seemed somewhat discombobulated. And I found it increasingly difficult to live up to a promise I had made. During our last conversation in his hospital room, Dad had made me vow I would help take care of Mom when he passed. "Since I will no longer be able to watch over your mother, I'm counting on you to carry the ball," he said.

When Dad uttered those words, I did not reply as a dutiful daughter should have. Instead I asked, "Why me? You have nine other children who are better prepared for that. Mom and I are like oil and water. We have no connection."

With a distraught look on his face, Dad replied, "I want you to promise me, right here and right now, girl."

And so, out of respect for my dying father, I merely shook my head in agreement.

As I ventured on a path to open my heart and forgive, I considered ways I might mend our fractured relationship. Because, if I was to be honest with myself, I would have to admit that the turmoil was as much my fault as it was Mom's. So as a means of expressing my emotions, I took the pen in hand and wrote a poem, one that I would later gift to Mom on Mother's Day.

A Mother's Love

As a small child, my mother's love appeared distant and cruel.
Distant, in the unreachable feelings

Cruel, in the reprimands of me
She seemed a sheltered woman
Driven hard in her need to be and remain cold

As a grown woman, my mother's love no longer eludes me
It shines in the depths of her eyes as she views me in her wisdom
It rings in the words that were once unheard
Why had they seemed unspoken
The love is felt in her touch as she hands me an insignificant item
I pause as her hand grazes mine
The warm feeling emits memories from a faded past

From a childhood when I was ill
Her soothing and her special songs
The way that she rocked me in the chair
Holding me to her breast as the pain eased away
I thought her love to be a forbidden fruit
A fruit that she refused to give

I now understand it was I who distanced myself
In my need to stress my independence
I stretched the plane of love to its outer bounds
Almost allowing it to become extinct, as an exotic animal or rare flower
It is timely that I have learned the truth of my mother's love
Before it was stilled for an eternity

My ability to love Mom more fully came when I finally understood that she had done the best she could. This did not occur to me until I became a mother myself. Although I had not made the same exact mistakes that Mom had, I had made my fair share. This newfound awareness led me to another of those illuminating moments, and I came to realize why Mom and I lacked a cohesive connection: I was bitter because I somehow felt that she had abandoned me, and that made it very hard for me to forgive.

Many years passed before we had the opportunity to fully heal our fractured relationship. And as with many revelations, it came in the most unexpected manner. At her invitation, I accompanied her to a healing mass that was offered at a local church by her parish priest. It was held on the third Thursday of each month and regardless of religious affiliation, all were welcome to attend. When Mom had first suggested that we go to the service, I was hesitant because by then, I no longer considered myself a traditional Catholic. Although I considered myself a religious person, my beliefs were centered more on spirituality than organized religion. I practiced daily prayer and meditation, I still believed in God, Jesus, the Blessed Mother, and the Holy Ghost, and my spiritual world also obviously embraced the angels. I could still feel my soul stir every time I prayed, and I still called to the Lord for His divine intervention. But I had little interest in attending a conventional religious service; I found that they usually left me feeling distracted and disconnected. However as requested, I went dutifully with Mom to the church.

Despite my reservations in attending the mass, it turned out to be an amazing experience. It provided us with a shared, miraculous moment of healing. The most significant moment came when the priest offered all in attendance the opportunity to receive some healing energy through the anointment of the Holy Spirit. As he dipped his finger in the oil and placed the symbolic sign of the cross upon my head, reciting a benediction in Latin, Mom unexpectedly took my hand in hers. I turned to look at her. My bewilderment must have shown on my face because she smiled, squeezed my hand, and a tear cascaded down her cheek. In that quiet moment, a spiritual experience took place. As the priest was bestowing his blessing on us at the altar, I felt the warmth of Mom's fingers move through the palm of my hand—the feeling unearthed a distant memory of her caring for me as a child. My mind recalled a time when I was suffering from an asthma attack and Mom had me cradled in her arms. As my head rested against her chest, she had sung a soft lullaby. I could hear the melody play in my mind all over again. I also remembered hearing the faint beating of her heart. And in that instant, it seemed that our heartbeats were synchronized as one again. I felt the primal force of motherhood transfer from her heart to mine: the consistent, drumming rhythm of a mother's heart in time with her daughter's.

In the soft surrender of the moment, I turned and looked at Mom and I sensed she somehow knew that something wonderful had occurred. Many had come to heal a weary body, but we had healed two tattered hearts. Our hearts had forgotten how to give and receive love, and how to forgive one another as well. But as Mom wrapped her hand in mine at the altar of our Lord, all of the pain and anger left me. The damaged fence between us was now mended, and the redemption and forgiveness that I had longed for finally manifested between us. That moment reminded me of the power of unconditional love between a mother and her child. Under the watchful eye of God and in His house of worship, I had found that love renewed.

THE FIRST VISITATION

Just a few months after Dad passed away, I had to undergo a hysterectomy. I was diagnosed with adenomyosis, a rare form of endometriosis. The disease had wreaked havoc inside my reproductive system. As I lay on the gurney in the hospital that cold, wintry day, I felt extremely anxious. It wasn't a normal feeling for me. In times of stress, I was generally calm and collected. I looked up at the anesthesiologist, who was already administering the drugs to make me sleep, and realized I needed to say something. I started to panic.

"I changed my mind about the surgery. I don't want to have it anymore," I said.

As I spoke those words, I was overcome by a deep sense of foreboding. In that minute fraction of time before I went under, I heard the voice again. It told me that there would be complications with the procedure. As I listened to the message play in my right ear, I felt so on edge. I believed that my angelic guide was trying to warn me of the difficulties that lay ahead of me. I attempted to lift myself up, and I felt the anesthesiologist press my body back down on the gurney. In a soft tone, the doctor tried to reassure me that I was just experiencing normal anxiety about having surgery, and he encouraged me to try and relax. He placed an oxygen mask on my face and asked me to count backward from 100. Within a few seconds, I succumbed to the effects of the drugs and fell asleep.

When I finally woke up after the surgery, I opened my eyes to see Mom and Vanessa in my hospital room. Vanessa was sitting in a chair next to the bed, and she had placed her head on my stomach. When she realized I was awake, she looked up at me. Her eyes were filled with tears. From the look on her face, I could tell she thought I might die.

It only took a few minutes for me to realize on my own that something had gone drastically wrong during the surgery. As I attempted to move slightly in the bed, a surge of excruciating pain ripped through my body. It was so intense that I almost lost consciousness. I asked Vanessa to call for help. A nurse was summoned and she immediately administered some medication, but it brought me little relief from the pain. When the surgeon arrived a short time later, he explained that my bladder had been punctured twice, and he was unsure if it would heal. He went on to explain that the injury brought a risk of infection, and that the next few days would be indicative of whether there would be any further complications.

When the doctor left the room, I looked at Vanessa. She was sobbing uncontrollably. Once again, Vanessa laid her head on my stomach. I could feel her body trembling as it pressed against me.

"Are you going to die?" she asked.

I smiled halfheartedly. "Only the good die young. And the last time I checked, I've not earned my wings."

The remark was my flippant attempt to make her laugh and calm down. However, it didn't work because in her eyes, I saw her fear. Vanessa was worried I might not make it. I realized then that I, too, shared the same fear. It had been only four months since Dad's death, and his passing still felt raw—I wasn't ready to confront my own mortality.

Two days later, my body could no longer fight the sepsis and the effects of the bacteria began to take their toll. In an attempt to rid my system of the microorganisms, the doctor administered some powerful medications to help fight the invading army of germs. All through that day, I was in a state of semiconsciousness. And although I was aware of my surroundings, I could hardly comprehend what was taking place. I could feel the weakening of my body. In reality, my cardiovascular system had collapsed—my veins were failing in their ability to hold the much-needed intravenous needles. As the nurse made repeated attempts to push the needle into my arms, I could feel my arms swelling and my mind slipping away. And when the nurse tried to poke the needle in my neck instead, I protested. I asked her not to touch my neck or to place a needle in it. At first, she disregarded my objections and continued in her attempts to find a vein. Yet as the nurse tried to find a vein in the contour of my neck, I again heard a voice whisper in my ear. It warned me not to allow the nurse to put the needle there. I demanded that she stop touching me; she left the room and said she was going to find the doctor.

When she left, I felt myself slipping further away and it seemed that I was entering into a state of altered consciousness. As my body's strength faded, I saw the apparition of my deceased father walk into the hospital room. He appeared handsome, healthy, and vibrant. His entire body was surrounded by a white light, just as Situ's had been. Dad smiled and extended his hand toward me.

"Girl, you are tired," he said. "Your heart is weak from all your years of pain and now the surgery has impaired your body even more. If you are ready to go, just grab ahold of my hand and I'll take you with me."

Dad's invitation was so warm and welcoming. Taking his hand would mean I could leave this earthly domain and experience no further suffering. But if I left with him, I would also be leaving Vanessa behind. I reached out to touch his hand. I longed to feel the comfort of one of his fatherly hugs. Yet, as I extended my hand toward my beloved patriarch, the image of Vanessa crying made me stop. I knew instinctively that it was not my time to go.

I smiled at Dad and said, "I'm not going anywhere until I have ten years by the beach with a nice man."

At my words, Dad pulled his hand away, smiled, and replied, "Then get up and fight."

As he uttered those five words of wisdom to me, the doctor entered the room and began to search my arm for a working vein. It only took him a single stab with a needle to find one ready to receive the life-giving drugs again. I watched the doctor gently holding my arm, and I could see that Dad continued to stand in my room, observing the activity taking place. Dad then gave me one last smile and left.

When Dad died, my greatest fear had been that I would never see him again. Yet in that inceptive moment of awareness, I knew that Dad would never really leave me. Although his human form was gone, his spirit had endured. He would remain an ever-shining beacon of light in not only my life, but in all his loved ones' as well.

CHAPTER 19

THE STORY OF A DAUGHTER FORETOLD

On a dreary winter's day, the white light of grace once again touched my life. The sky was overcast and drizzly and there was a chill in the air. Vanessa was on her way to the hospital. It appeared she was in labor, even though it was three weeks before her due date.

As I made my way to the hospital, I began to feel a bit anxious. Over the previous week, Vanessa had experienced some health issues relating to high blood pressure and edema. As a result, she had gained significant water weight and was beginning to suffer from preeclampsia. When I arrived, a nurse was taking Vanessa's vitals. From the look on her face, I could tell something was amiss. The nurse indicated that Vanessa's blood pressure was extremely elevated and that her present condition could cause both her and the unborn child some possible health risks. Vanessa was placed on her side in an inverted position on a specialized hospital bed. As I watched from a short distance away, I became even more concerned about her welfare and the baby's. After all, it is never an easy task to watch your own child suffer. In that moment, my mind regressed once again to Vanessa as a helpless child, and as one impression after the other entered my mind, I was reminded once again of our unique bond.

After she was settled into the room, Vanessa asked me to go back to her house and pick up some personal items that she had forgotten in her rush to get to the hospital. I protested. I didn't want to leave her side, but she assured me that she and the baby were in good hands.

On the way, I made a brief stop at the cemetery to visit my father's grave. I parked my car and walked over to his plot. I touched the gravestone. I thought about how much I wished Dad could be there. Although he had had some issues with Vanessa's choices, Dad loved children. I knew he would have welcomed the baby with open arms. I stood there praying for Dad's immortal soul. As I did, I asked Daddy to go to the ear of God and ask Him to protect Vanessa and the unborn grandchild. I prayed for divine intervention. Just as I said my last amen, I felt the rain stop. I noticed that the sun was beginning to shine through the gray clouds. I raised my face toward the heavens and allowed myself to feel its warmth. Between the solace of the cemetery and the sun's heat, I felt a momentary sense of peace.

As I stood there gazing at the sunlight, a lovely, misty-pink cloud appeared above me. Although it was small, its colors were brilliant, especially in contrast to the gray clouds above. The rosy-hued mass moved ever so slowly across the sky. As I peered at the cloud, I heard the familiar angelic voice whisper in my ear, "All is well."

When I heard the words, I desperately wanted to believe them to be true. I wanted so much for my child and grandchild to be healthy and safe. Before too long, the cloud disappeared from the sky and a light drizzle began again. I left the cemetery feeling much calmer than when I had arrived.

After retrieving Vanessa's belongings, I returned to the hospital. I related my experience at Dad's grave.

"Do you think it was a sign?" she asked.

Before I had a chance to respond to her question, an elderly relative who was present in the room—the grandmother of the baby's father—interjected, "It is the soul of your baby girl arriving on this earth."

Vanessa and I smiled. Both of us seemed to resonate with the statement, and we hoped her words would hold true.

A few grueling hours later, our newest member of the family arrived. She was a beautiful little girl with a very thick head of coal-black hair and large, almond-shaped eyes. We were all grateful for her safe arrival. Not so long after the birth, Vanessa's blood pressure lowered and the inflammation decreased. It was a great relief to know her health was no longer at risk and that all *was* indeed well.

The next morning while watching television, I heard the newscaster describe innumerable sightings of small blue-and-pink clouds floating across the skies of the United States. All of the eyewitness accounts had indicated that the clouds were very unusual in color, shape, and movement. I smiled to myself. I thought there must have been many new babies delivered to Earth yesterday. I knew that these little ones had arrived riding on the wings of the angels. Each had a guardian who brought them safely to this domain. In my heart, I looked forward to the day when my granddaughter would be old enough to hear the story of the day she was born. I couldn't wait to describe to her how she arrived on Earth gliding across the sky on a small pink-hued cloud and guided by the wings of an angel.

As I stood next to Vanessa immediately following the birth, I admired the lovely face of her child. It was one of those rare moments in one's life that is forever etched on the heart. Despite the exquisite happiness of the moment, I couldn't help but think about my family members who were not there. The moment was bittersweet. Due to the ongoing issues relating to the interracial coupling, familial relationships were still somewhat strained.

In the weeks leading up to my granddaughter's birth, I had read a magazine article in either *Discovery* or *Psychology Today* that addressed the physical and emotional development of multicultural children. It addressed both the positives and the negatives. The words of that article held great meaning for me. My responsibility as a grandmother, I realized, would be doubly significant for this child: if I was to be effective in my new granddaughter's life, it would be necessary for me to impart guidance and wisdom, too.

With the arrival of my first grandchild came the heightened sensation of my heart opening again after my father's death. In my years, I have experienced my share of emotional attachments. But the instantaneous connection I felt with my granddaughter was different. I was amazed at how easily our relationship seemed to form. Yet despite the bliss I felt, it did not take long before I began to fret about the baby's well-being. Try as I might, I found it difficult to remove worry from my mind. When I recalled a dream of long ago, from the night before Vanessa was born, however, a sense of peace and wonder took hold of me. And I found that that past vision comforted and reminded me that all had been foretold.

My vivid dream was about Vanessa and what was yet to be. I saw the birth of a baby girl and the many chapters of her life play out before my eyes. I watched each detail as if it were projected across a movie screen. The dream unnerved me in some way at the time because I wasn't sure if it was a real vision of my future. In the dream, the little girl was about two to three years in age, with lovely straight blond hair the color of summer straw. She had piercing blue eyes the color of a brilliant topaz gemstone. Her eyes were almond shaped with long, flowing lashes. She was wearing a printed turquoise top and matching pants. Although small in stature, she carried an air of confidence about her. And she was seated in a chair as if posing for a photograph.

The next part of the dream involved another little girl. By the pale brown tone of her skin color, she appeared to be of biracial ethnicity. She had short, dark brown, curly hair. Her eyes were amber and were almond shaped, just like those of the first child in my vision.

The last part of the dream featured my mother and me. We were seated in an auditorium with another woman who bore similar features to us. We were all there watching a young, biracial woman on a stage. My mother was much older in age in the dream than she actually was at the time. And the woman next to me I guessed to be about 40. When I took an even closer look at us, I saw that I, too, was much older than I was at the time. I looked to be about 60 years of age.

In my dream, I heard a man's voice whisper to me, "This is your daughter and these are the stories of your life."

I woke up from the dream feeling calmer about the impending birth. The foreboding mood that had taken hold of me some months prior had now dissipated. It was replaced by a serenity I had not felt prior to falling asleep. Unbeknownst to me at the time, the dream sequence was a gift from my guardian angel. Archangel Michael was once again placing my spirit at ease.

The night passed into the next day, and I gave birth to a daughter with dark black hair and almond shaped, blue eyes. Over the next few months, her hair changed to a blond hue similar to that of straw.

Many years later, when my own daughter gave birth to her little girl, my first granddaughter, she was indeed biracial. As she grew into a toddler, her hair changed to a lovely chestnut brown color highlighted with auburn. Her eyes were amber, with flecks of gold in the irises. Her skin was a lovely light brown that reflected the heritage of both her races.

The last sequence of that dream was of my eldest granddaughter taking the stage at her senior prom. Standing there in a flowing gown of teal hues, she stood smiling proudly. And in the audience next to me sat my mother, to my left, and Vanessa, to my right.

Amazingly, the dream had in fact foretold the future. Those visions, in fact, taught me to better trust my intuition. In the years that followed that initial glimpse of my life to be, I came to fully embrace the messages and impressions that arrived when I slumbered. I have now come to better understand how deeply I am interconnected with those I love most.

When I am but a distant memory, I want my granddaughter to hear my words whispering in the wind. I hope she will understand their meaning when she begins to reflect on her own past and the significant moments and persons who aided her on her journey to adulthood. In her quiet moments of reflection, I pray she will hear my words of wisdom resound in her mind and let them find a home in her heart—just as my grandmother's words found a place in mine. And in the worst moments of my granddaughter's life, I pray she hears the angelic beings as they whisper in her ear, "All is well."

CHAPTER 20

MY HEART
IS IN FULL BLOOM

When my granddaughter was nine months old, Vanessa asked if she and the little one could move back home. After a few tough years of trying, Vanessa's relationship with the child's father had gone from bad to worse. Before too long, we were living together again in a lovely red brick home in close proximity to several of our family members. It didn't take much time for us to adjust to the new lifestyle and to begin to enjoy each other's company and support.

The first summer living in the house together, I decided to landscape the yard and fill it with flowers. I loved the beauty of blossoms, with their brilliant colors and fragrant scents. A flower received always seemed to brighten one's day, so I thought it would be nice to look out the windows and see a spread laid out across the green of the lawn. My grandmother Situ had loved flowers as well. She had a beautiful rose garden in her yard, and a green thumb when it came to anything she placed in the soil. Rosebushes of many colors were nestled around the borders of her yard, and they enhanced the quaintness of her home. Anyone who visited Situ admired the landscape and felt their warm embrace—and the love they portrayed.

I can recall on many a youthful summer's evening gazing out my bedroom window, located directly across the street from Situ's yard. She would often be standing in her own little patch of Heaven on Earth. Whenever Situ was gardening or breathing in the fragrance of a flower, I could see a smile illuminate her face. It was a look of sheer and utter contentment. That smile still lingers inside my mind. Situ had an endearing grin that warmed the best parts of my heart and made me glad she was in my life. It was an amazing feature that provided a glimpse into the depths of my grandmother's soul.

Years later, when I visited a botanical garden near Niagara Falls, I saw a sign displayed in a flower bed that read: "Flowers are God's embroidery on Earth." And so it was with Situ's garden beds. There in her yard, she had sowed and reaped a harvest of her love. She created a beautiful garden that embroidered the earth in a spectrum of vibrant colors. It was a symbol of her love for God's earth. In a way, planting a garden of my own would be a way for me to honor Situ—a woman who had beautified the earth and had etched memories on my heart as well.

With each patch of dirt lifted from the ground, the garden began to take shape as I toiled in the soil. I cut the small garden into the shape of a heart and encircled it with red bricks to match my house. I decided to give the garden a name that would express the way I felt about Vanessa and my granddaughter, so I dubbed it, "My Heart Is in Full Bloom." This name captured the way that I felt when I looked at them. In time, my granddaughter began to help me tend the garden that symbolized our family's love. I enjoyed watching her dig up the ground, plant seeds, and water delicate new blooms. I found such delight in teaching her and watching her partake in a hobby that we both seemed to enjoy.

Many years have passed since that first season of blooms, and I have continued to tend to the small patch of earth with great care. In the summer of 2009, when it was once again time to plant flowers in the heart-shaped garden, I decided to plant a dark pink dianthus to symbolize Vanessa's love for her now-expanded family. I planted deep red dianthus in each corner around that, which represented my grandchildren. This was done to signify that each child shared a part of their mother's heart and that she, in turn, was surrounded by their love as well. Around the border of the garden, I planted alyssum to express my love. The alyssum would spread around the edges of the lovely little flowerets, merging with and enhancing the other blossoms. Every time I looked out at the garden that year, I was reminded of the love I felt for my family.

As life passes by and summers come and go all too quickly, the heart-shaped garden is a constant reminder of our special love. It represents the impressions of a heart that is indeed in full bloom. Its effervescent blooms remind me of my love for a daughter and the grandchildren who have grounded me on this earth. Just like the flowers and the soil, our bond is sustained through constant nurturing and grooming. And just like the perennials that begin to grow in the early summer months, my grandchildren continue to grow under the watchful eye of their mother, who keeps them centered, and their grandmother, who helps to provide wisdom.

Long after I am gone, it is my hope that the memory of the heart-shaped garden will remain inside my grandchildren's hearts and minds. I hope that just as the perennials bloom each summer, so will my legacy of love. May it be perpetually engraved in their hearts. As each future summer arrives and they see blooms around them, may they remember me gardening, as I have recollected my Situ. May each tiny seed they place into the ground bloom as the sun shines down upon it—and them as well. May their efforts spread to become an embroidered patch of delight for all to enjoy. May the garden open up *their* hearts into full bloom, just as it did mine all of those years ago. And when it is their turn to go, may they leave behind their own legacy of grace, honor, and love, as I hope I have done for them.

CHAPTER 21

THE BLUE MAN

Over time, Vanessa and I found that living in the same house sometimes placed a strain on our relationship. The fact that Vanessa was dealing with a broken heart did not help matters. The stress of juggling that, working a full-time job, and the baby took its toll on Vanessa, and she was sometimes distant. However, the living situation had a very different effect on the relationship I shared with my granddaughter. She and I bonded in a very special way. We grew very close, and she became a very important part of my life.

As she grew from an infant into a toddler, she began to talk to what appeared to be an imaginary friend. On occasion, when I would ask her who she was talking to, she would smile and say, "The Blue Man."

When my granddaughter was five years of age, I had the opportunity to travel with her and Vanessa to South Carolina. Vanessa was scheduled to attend a training conference in Columbia, South Carolina, but she did not like flying. We decided to take the drive south together.

While Vanessa attended her training sessions, my granddaughter and I visited several different places: Charleston, Myrtle Beach, and the small barrier islands just off the coast.

On one particular night, as she and I were traveling back to our hotel after dropping off Vanessa at the training site, we got lost. At first I tried not to alarm my grandchild, but after a while, I think she sensed my concern.

All at once, she calmly said, "I'm not scared. The angel is with us, and he's talking to me. He told me that as soon as you pass over the railroad tracks you will know where to go."

I asked her to describe the angel who was in the car with us.

"It's the Blue Man who I see and talk to all the time."

I turned to look at her. Her beautiful little face was smiling back at me. In just a few miles, we crossed over a set of railroad tracks and saw a road sign that indicated we were going in the right direction after all.

As we continued our drive back to the hotel, she told me more about the Blue Man. She explained that he was very handsome, large in size, spoke with a soft voice, and glowed with his blue light. She said she talked with him quite often, and he always seemed to be near when she needed a friend. With each piece of information she related, it became more and more apparent to me that the Blue Man in question was Archangel Michael. I was elated that he was now watching over my lovely little granddaughter. It was very comforting and reassuring to know she, too, believed in angels and was seeing our family's divine protector. I knew with Michael by her side she would be safe, and that he would provide her with the protection she would need as she traveled through the phases of her life. It was a moment of utter and complete satisfaction for me.

When we arrived back at the hotel, I lifted my little darling girl from her seat and kissed her ever so softly on her brow. She was already fast asleep. I could feel the warmth of her body and she was snoring softly with each breath. My blood ebbed and flowed as the dance of life between a grandmother and a grandchild began again. My life was indeed blessed and I gave thanks to God for her presence. It was at that point I became keenly aware about the generations of my family who shared a propensity for seeing the angels.

I also recollected the story of grace that my dad had often shared with his children. Dad had told us that if we behaved in an appropriate manner and did not intentionally hurt others, we would earn grace in our lives. In turn, this blessing would be bestowed upon three generations of the family: the older generation would take care of the present, and the present generation paved the way for the future generation. As I pondered Dad's words in that quiet moment of reflection, I realized he had indeed been right. Although our family had experienced its share of problems, it surely seemed blessed. Each time an unhappy incident or event brought some bad news or created a negative situation, the family would bounce back and become even stronger. Somehow, in our family, each generation had been provided with the grace our forebears had bestowed upon it. As time marched on and our family tree grew, the favor came full circle. The stories my Situ had shared with me about our Khouri ancestry resounded again in my ear. Her words of wisdom were a reminder to me that I must conduct myself in a manner respectful of the past generations of our family. Not only did my own spiritual growth depend upon my behavior, but generations yet to be were counting on me, too.

I now realize that the expression "the sins of the father" does not imply that my children or their children's children will merely be punished for my bad deeds—a negative family legacy runs much deeper and affects the very basics of our humanity. I believe that if we do not teach our children well or assist them in becoming functional and spiritual human beings, they in turn will not be able to provide an adequate tutelage to their children. Dysfunction will prevail and the family will not be equipped to thrive during times of challenge. As my mind twisted with these thoughts, I once again felt deep gratitude to God for sending Archangel Michael to watch over our family and to extend his hand to us in guiding us through the murky waters of life.

Many years later, the Blue Man took on a new dimension in my life. The day after Christmas in 2010, my mom had come to my house for our annual holiday luncheon. She and I chatted for a bit and then she asked me a question about what I was writing.

"Are any of the chapters in your book about me?" she asked.

"Yes," I replied.

Mom continued, "Did you write anything negative about me?"

I was somewhat stunned at her question and responded, "Well, no."

Mom half-smiled at my reply.

"Would you like me to read to you what I wrote about us?" I asked.

She answered, "Yes, I would."

So I spent the next few minutes reading to her. When I was finished, Mom said to me, "Thank you for telling the truth about us and for not hurting me in any way."

I didn't know what to say or do. So we sat there in my kitchen in silence for a few minutes. Each of us was lost in our own thoughts about the other. When Mom did finally speak again, she asked me, "Do you still see angels?"

I was shocked at her question. "Yes," I replied, somewhat dumbfounded.

"Do you still see the Blue Man with wings?"

This question, too, threw me off for a moment. "How do you know about the Blue Man?" I asked.

"When you were a little girl, you used to come downstairs late at night and tell your father and me that a blue man with wings was in your bedroom. We would tell you there was nothing there, but you were always insistent he was real. Sometimes, Daddy would take you back upstairs to your bedroom and look under the bed and in the closet to try and reassure you that no one was there. But you were convinced that, despite our not being able to see him, the Blue Man truly existed. And, on occasion, you would be insistent that he was standing in the corner of your room, all the while smiling at you and surrounded by blue light."

When Mom finished telling me that story from my childhood, my eyes welled up with tears. "Why haven't you ever told me this story? If I had known sooner, my gift might not have felt so strange."

"When you were growing up, people just didn't acknowledge visions or angelic beings. If they did, others would have thought them to be mentally ill. I was trying to protect you."

I said, "Mom, do you know that my granddaughter sees the Blue Man? She often tells me about how he visits with her when she feels afraid or alone. Isn't that something?"

"You are both blessed," Mom replied.

We sat there for a few moments more without saying another word; we just reflected on our conversation. For me, it was heartwarming to have Mom finally acknowledge the existence of the Archangel Michael. It had been a long time coming. As my mother left my home that day, I gave her a big hug and thanked her. She looked at me in a quizzical manner.

"You helped me to remember the very first times I saw my beloved angelic friend," I said. "It has all come full circle, and now I know the truth of the matter. Since I was a child, I have had visions of the Archangel and to know you were aware of it helps me finally make sense of it all."

I gave Mom another hug and she got into her car. As she pulled away, I felt a great sense of relief fill my soul. I had shared a good day with Mom and we had one of those precious moments that brings about peaceful resolution to matters of the heart. My belief in God and His angelic realm was also reaffirmed. Somewhere deep inside my soul, I sensed I now had Mom's blessing. The Bible references the importance of a parent's favor to their child. In my heart, I felt that Mom had finally accepted my belief in the angels, the celestial beings who had provided so much grace not only in my life, but in our entire family's as well.

CHAPTER 22

THE TWO FACES OF MICHAEL

As I move through my personal journey and continue to search for the answers to my questions, Archangel Michael continues to be a beacon of light. But there is another Michael, a man who has also played a significant role in my life. The story of Michael is a cherished one for me.

I first met Michael when I was 16 years old. He was sitting on my parents' porch discussing football with Dad. At the time, Dad was coaching a semiprofessional football team and Michael was their running back. When I saw him, I thought he was the most handsome of men. His smile melted my heart immediately. In those first few moments, I felt my spirit merge with his. It was as though we already knew one another. But given that I was a married woman at the time, I kept my distance and politely retreated back into the house. There, in the stillness of the kitchen, I caught my breath. And for a moment, my mind traveled to some unknown space where my spirit seemed to linger for some time. It somehow felt as if there was a distant memory of him trying to find its path to my conscious mind.

Although I periodically watched Michael playing football, years passed before I had the occasion to actually speak to him again. I ran into him at a nightclub, and I was there with several family members after attending a wedding. We were all out on the floor dancing and enjoying the evening. When I noticed Michael sitting at the bar, he looked up and smiled. My heart leapt. Our eyes met for a brief second before I quickly turned away. It somehow felt as if he could peer inside my mind and read my very thoughts. I knew my heart rate had increased and I could feel my face begin to flush. I felt a connection to him and heard his spirit calling to mine. It took everything inside me not to run to him. As I stood there wondering what to do, he walked right up to me and said, "Hello."

With that one simple word, he took my breath away. For a brief moment, I felt the entire roomful of people disappear. It was just the two of us standing on the dance floor. I felt the room begin to spin. As I looked into his deeply set, dark-brown eyes, I felt an unfamiliar stirring. I became lost in the wonder of him and in his scent, too. No other man had ever enticed my sense of smell like him. The memory of our first dance is forever embedded in my mind. When he placed his hand in mine, it felt as if we merged as one. His touch felt incredible, and my entire being delighted in the sensation. My heart pulsed in a rhythmic beat as it connected to his. Our feet moved in synchronicity to the music, and our minds did the same. I swear I could already hear the words he was going to say. When the song ended, I pulled away in haste. Although I was very unhappy in my marriage, I had made a commitment and felt obligated to honor my vows.

Some years after my marriage ended, Michael and I became acquainted again. We wound up reuniting and separating numerous times, in fact. Despite our long-standing love affair, we were never able to get it quite right. I've often wondered why that was. It seemed the problem had to do with timing—not just physical, but emotional. Although we had an intense spiritual connection, our minds and hearts always failed to synchronize as one.

During the initial years of our relationship, I admit that I had a difficult time overcoming the difference in our races. I feared my father's reaction to my desire to spend my life with a man of color, especially after having experienced so much familial discord around Vanessa's relationship. Michael, too, seemed wary of an interracial relationship and the disapproval of his loved ones. Our relationship also suffered because of Michael's behavior. He had a propensity for violence and was known around the community for his ill temper. He also had a reputation for being quite the "ladies' man."

However, as I grew to know him better, I realized that Michael's behavior had much to do with his childhood circumstances. Unlike me, he did not have a nurturing family to provide him with security. His family dynamic often caused him to act out in a negative manner. Through my work with child victims, I was knowledgeable about the long-term psychological effects abuse and/or neglect could cause to a child. I came to realize that Michael was driven by demons related to his upbringing.

One day, I heard a whisper in my ear tell me that I needed to help Michael. I decided to give him three books: a Bible, *The Last of the Mohicans*, and *Sonnets from the Portuguese*. I chose the Bible so he might learn about God and know he was dearly loved despite his flaws. *The Last of the Mohicans* would serve as an example of a warrior who chose the path of peace despite living in a tumultuous world.

The last book, *Sonnets from the Portuguese*, was chosen so he would know a love worth having was worth nurturing.

When I gave him the books, I saw tears form in his eyes. He confessed that no one had ever been concerned about his emotional welfare, nor had anyone tried to guide him in a positive direction. As he finished talking, I whispered a silent prayer. I asked God to help Michael become the man he was meant to be.

Michael remains very close to my heart. He was present at many important events in my life. When none of my family members would come to the hospital to meet Vanessa's baby girl, Michael showed up, flashing his familiar smile.

A few hours following my first granddaughter's birth, he and I discussed our relationship. He talked about all the issues we faced, and we agreed that even though we might not be able to change the past, we did have hope for the future. Michael implied that the birth of my granddaughter had brought a transformation into all our lives. When he finished speaking, my eyes filled with tears and a rush of emotion overcame me. And once again, his heart synchronized with mine and the world felt right for a little while. I was comforted by his presence and my soul was at peace.

Some years later, Michael came back into my life—by arriving at my home unexpectedly. As he stood there in the entryway, my heart sang out with joy. My arms reached out to embrace him. My mind transcended to a place of pure contentment where only the soul dwells. Despite distance and a lapsing of time, our feelings seemed unchanged. It felt as if no time had passed and he had always been a consistent part of my life. My soul rejoiced in his presence, and my heart opened up in a moment of pure revelation.

During the time we spent together then, Michael encountered the Archangel. One night, he awoke and went into the kitchen to get a drink of water. A few minutes later, I thought I heard him mumbling something about a blue light. At the time, I did not fully comprehend what he was saying because I was half-asleep. In the morning, he told me he had witnessed a large, blue, illuminated shape standing in the kitchen corner.

"What does this mean?" he asked.

I explained that apparently Archangel Michael had manifested himself, and that he was always near me and had been for most of my life. For whatever reason, the angelic being had decided to appear to Michael. I reassured him that this was a gift from the highest power, and I told him he should feel honored to have seen the Archangel. Although I did my best to reassure Michael about the angelic encounter, I wondered why the Archangel might have chosen to present himself just then.

I was eager to learn more about the Archangel's appearance that night, so I asked Michael about the shape and size of the blue light. He told me the blue light was much larger in stature than he was. He was not quite sure of its exact shape, though, because he had instinctively turned away from it. His fear of the unknown had caused him to look away.

I tried to get him to be more descriptive about what he saw, and even brought a few items for him to look at. When I placed an Archangel Michael oracle card in front of him, he hesitated for a moment, and then shook his head no. It was clear to me that he was fearful of the unknown and not comfortable discussing it. He said he had a blue shirt the same color as the apparition, though, and he hurriedly went to retrieve the garment. When he laid it on the kitchen table, it was obvious to me that the color matched the oracle card. It was a deep cobalt blue. I once again took the Archangel Michael card from its box and laid it on the shirt. As I did, his eyes filled with tears.

As we chatted more about the Archangel and his appearance in my kitchen, Michael became nervous. I tried to put his mind at ease. "The angels are present in our lives to do only good," I said. "They are the bearers of light and love. They are God's messengers."

As we spoke, he began to open up and tell me about the times when he had thought about us and our inability to fully embrace our relationship. He confessed that, on occasion, he would close his eyes and attempt to travel to me. In his mind, he would place himself in the corner of my bedroom or by my couch in the living room. He said he wanted to watch over me. It occurred to me that the two locations Michael had identified were the very places where the Archangel Michael had stood when he visited me. And I realized that, at those times, the Archangel was not only soothing me, but doing the same for Michael. Through extraordinary means, this wonderful angelic being was helping Michael and me to remain linked in spirit.

During those few days of rediscovery and recapturing our memories—both good and bad—Michael and I apologized to each other for all of our past indiscretions. Those apologies came with an outpouring of emotion that words cannot describe. Our bruised minds and tainted hearts were healed, and we saw that the reality of our situation was truly linked of spirit.

I have come to realize that Michael stands clearly in my mind as the most significant man with whom I have shared my heart. Michael's love has had an everlasting effect on me. He has a prominent place inside the endless boundaries of my heart, and the love I've felt for him intertwines with the love I've felt for Dad, Mom, Vanessa, and my grandchildren. Even if he and I never find our happy ending, we have still found our happily ever after: we have the comfort of knowing the other exists and will be there when the other is in need. He remains the missing half of my being, despite our long-standing inability to fully commit. Perhaps sometime in the distant future we will get this relationship right. I sustain my life by hoping for that. For when true love is obtained, even in the simplest of forms, its power is limitless.

So I have discovered that my life has been graced by these two faces of Michael. The Archangel Michael has served as my celestial guide. He is here to provide me with protection and to assist me in fulfilling my life's purpose. The Archangel has always been—and continues to be—my connection to God and His universal energy and light. Michael the man is my earthly connection to my humanity. He is here to remind me that, although I am a spiritual being, I am also a human, and my time on Earth is limited. He reminds me to experience and learn about the wonders this life has to offer. Michael has grounded me and provided me with kindred fellowship and with courage. And I now understand he is the only one of my romantic liaisons who has gifted me with ongoing, unconditional love.

The two faces of Michael—one angelic and one human—have provided me with the strength to continue on and fulfill God's plan for me. They both have shared the position of being my guardian angel in life. Under their watchful eyes, I have grown into a strong and resilient woman who is knowledgeable of self, of spirit, and of my fellow man.

CHAPTER 23

THE ART OF
KYTHING

In the weeks that followed Michael's return and the Archangel's manifestation, I tried to find the meaning behind what had transpired. But try as I might, none of the logical reasons that my mind conjured up made any sense. I found myself wondering how or why the three of us were connected as one. Although I had complete faith in the Archangel, his possible reasons for appearing that night eluded me.

Like any other trained investigator, I felt the need to find a rational explanation. I did not yet fully understand the concept of channeling—opening communications between the angelic realm and the earthly realm—or the connections that can occur because of it. Even though I felt comfortable in my own direct communication with angels, the concept of simultaneously connecting with another human being was not easy for me to comprehend, let alone accept.

At first I was perplexed by the very concept, and my linear mind worked feverishly to analyze the known facts about it. As my ability to channel with the angelic realm heightened and it became clear that the celestial beings operated outside the constraints of the physical world, I began to question the reality of the situation and, on some occasions, my own sanity as well. Was it really the angels communicating with me? Or was I going mad? After repeated discussions with a psychologist, I became more comfortable with the idea that I had gifts and accepted that my clairaudience, clairsentience, and clairvoyance had evolved to a higher level. Although the practice of channeling cannot be explained logically, I am convinced it is a divine mystery and originates from God.

One day as I sat talking with a close friend who also happened to be a mental health practitioner, I learned a new term that helped me to better understand my experiences. While she was relating a revelatory occurrence that had happened in her life, she mentioned the word *kything*. When I confessed that I was unfamiliar with the word, she seemed surprised. She explained that the term applied to an individual's ability to conduct distant communication with another, without any direct contact. After listening to her explain it more fully, I had an epiphany of sorts. I became convinced that through some form of kything and the aid of the Archangel, Michael and I were able to communicate.

In order to become better acquainted with this phenomenon, I conducted some research. What I found was that kything is a wordless, mind-to-mind communication in which one person essentially *becomes* another, seeing through their eyes and feeling through their senses. The two people intuitively know the meaning of what the other is telling them, without relying on such things as words or pictures. In essence, it is a sense of presence without space, time, or relative size, and it is based on the concept of oneness, which states that all that exists is one.

After reading the definition, I felt better able to understand the interconnectivity.

Through the angel's eyes, I have been able to see the miracles in lives both past and present. Through his voice, I have been afforded the opportunity to hear his messages. It also gave credence to the angelic encounter that I witnessed at the Flight 93 crash site on 9/11. As the motion of each movement of the angels recorded in my mind on that fateful day, it paused and paced itself in slow motion, before my very eyes. I am now keenly aware that what transpired had everything to do with the process of kything. For those brief few minutes, my mind quieted down to a slower rhythm that allowed for it to fully observe, grasp, and memorize all that was occurring. The details of the events were then planted inside my subconscious mind. And they waited there until I was prepared to give testimony.

This newfound knowledge about kything also helped me to understand the connections I had shared with those I loved. Over the years, my mind had bonded both with the Archangel and with several beloved individuals. When I first became aware of this miraculous ability, I was riddled with fear. As a child, I was scolded for my overactive imagination. As I grew into adolescence, I never felt as if I fit in with the rest of the world. And as an adult, I would sometimes feel very disconnected with the world and many of the people in it. The type of close relationships I tended to make usually stayed intact for long periods of time, and this fact gave rise to my belief that everyone in our lives serves a purpose. Some stay only for short periods. Some arrive at intermittent times. And then there are those special people who find a place in our hearts and remain there for the rest of our lives. And, if we pay close attention, we will have the opportunity to learn valuable lessons from them. Each of my closest relationships is based on sharing a connection that confirms my belief that individuals' souls can be linked. However, when life becomes stressful, we tend to block that connection. The remedy is to stop, breathe, and listen. For in the listening comes the connection to each other and to the Divine.

CHAPTER 24

THE EYES
ARE THE MIRROR
OF THE SOUL

When I was a young woman, I would often sit with Situ on her back porch. There among her lovely flower beds, with a cup of coffee in hand, she and I had the opportunity to discuss many subjects about life. Each time we talked, I learned more about the history of our family and new and interesting topics. For a woman with little formal education, my grandmother had an innate ability when it came to the observation of human nature. During one of our talks, she spoke about a subject that piqued my curiosity: how the eyes were the mirror of an individual's soul. At first, I was just overwhelmed by the magnitude of her wisdom. But as she began to explain what she meant in detail and to instruct me, I began to see how reading other people's eyes could open me up to better understanding humanity. She told me that each person's eyes tell a story worth learning and that when you are able to look deep inside and to reach through that mirror, their tale would unfold. She provided me with a wealth of information about how a simple iris could reflect the truth about someone's life, health, and emotions.

The coloration of an iris and its variations reflect the sum of a person's experience. She explained that one area of the eye holds a trace of innocence. Another displays emotional balance and stability. A different portion depicts kindness or cruelty. Yet another section reveals deep and traumatic pain and sometimes even addiction. And if you look deep enough into the iris, it answers all the questions you might have about someone, and reveals a truth or a lie. As my grandmother continued with her repertoire, some of it began to make sense to me. At the end of our conversation, I thanked her for the guidance bestowed and embraced her theory with fervor. However, it would take years before I would fully comprehend the concept of iridology. It came only after practicing the theory and developing an uncanny ability to read others.

At first I would only occasionally and casually test my grandmother's concept about the eyes. I would look at the irises of family members and study them when they spoke. I'd watch as they laughed and told stories about themselves. I would ask them questions and try to determine if they were telling the truth or lying. It was a wonderful experiment in learning more about them—and about human nature as well. But it wasn't until my early days of policing that the practice of iridology became a functional part of my daily life. With each new case I investigated, I began to study the eyes of the suspect. Encountering offenders on a regular basis gave me the opportunity to study the mirrored soul theory in depth. I found that many of those arrested did uphold my grandmother's teachings on iridology. When I patrolled the streets, I often put her theories into practice as well. I learned to test another person's intentions by reading the iris. In them, I would instantly be able to assess the level of threat or danger to myself or to others. I became keenly aware of their behavioral intent by watching instantaneous changes unfold around the pupils of their eyes. It was amazing to me how well the eyes foretold any actions someone was about to take. In them, I could detect anger, hurt, or detachment. Detachment was always the most worrisome to me, because a person who could disconnect from his or her own feelings during an altercation was a person who would have no problem inflicting great pain on another. In the few times that I recognized this trait in an individual, I felt chills run up my back to my neck—another intuitive warning that I learned to heed.

As I advanced in my career, I became even more interested in the inner workings of the mind and how the eyes could tell someone's tale. I read books on the subjects of body language and iridology to better understand what they revealed about the mind and the inner emotions that lay hidden in its cave. I pursued every avenue that was permissible in order to study an adversary's eyes. In times of great strife in my life, I have learned to rely on my judgment in reading eyes, for in the blink of one, an entire story can unfold. I have found iridology to be an effective tool for gaining knowledge about the important persons in my life as well. I can immediately detect an illness in my daughter and her children or read their emotional state on any given day. Their eyes hold the truth of their current well-being. As I peer into the beautiful hues of my family's eyes, it becomes possible for me to observe the swirling magic of their minds and the secrets they hold dear to their hearts as well. Vanessa even once told her eldest daughter, "Cover your eyes if you're going to lie to Mom, because she knows when you are being less than honest."

Some of the men I have worked with over the years have become wary when they talk with me, too. I've heard it stated on more than one occasion: "Next time we talk, I'm wearing a pair of sunglasses to cover my eyes!"

I once had the chance to discuss the concept of iridology with a polygrapher who worked for the FBI. He first explained the various ways a polygraph instrument was capable of detecting a lie. I listened carefully. Then I shared with him what I knew about iridology. During our conversation, he asked if I would be willing to demonstrate my technique on him. I agreed. I searched his eyes for information, and after just a brief assessment, I began to tell him the story of his life. I told him about his childhood, his father, his fears, and his personality, too. I provided him with details I would never have known. Before too long, he indicated he had heard enough and admitted that iridology held some merit. I was grateful to him for his willingness to be objective.

In retrospect, I can see how our conversation brought awareness to me as well as to him. Situ had provided me with a skill many years before my talk with that man, but trying it on someone who usually relied on scientific methods proved that it worked. I was confident she had taught me well. My grandmother had such an uncanny ability to read people. I was grateful she taught me a skill that became a valuable tool for my profession, and for my personal life as well.

As my family members and acquaintances alike have learned, the eye is a deep sea filled with knowledge, and its intricate patterns can relay intimate details about a person. Over the many years since my grandmother first shared her ability with me as we sat on her back porch, I have come to a fuller understanding of the iris's connection to the mind, the heart, and the soul. And I've resolved that it is indeed true—the eyes are the mirror of the soul.

CHAPTER 25

THE G-MEN
CAME CALLING

In 1997, my career took a sudden and unexpected turn. While I enjoyed my position on the college campus police department, the job had lost its luster. I longed for something more challenging. I was also an instructor for the United States Attorney's Office, Western District of Pennsylvania, at the time. As a member of that prestigious training team, I was afforded the opportunity to collaborate with an amazing group of talented professionals. We traveled together to numerous cities across the country and instructed law enforcement officers, social service practitioners, elected officials, school administrators, educators, and community members on a myriad of topics. During one of these training sessions, I met a man who would challenge me to take a bold step forward. As I was busily preparing to instruct a lesson, I turned to find an unfamiliar man standing at the podium. He smiled and introduced himself. He complimented me on my relatable teaching style and humorous delivery. He then asked a surprising question: "Why aren't you working for the FBI?"

I smiled and flippantly responded, "When you find the FBI, how about telling them where I am?"

Without missing a beat, I turned away from him. I was therefore unaware that the man had left his business card lying on the dais. When I turned back around, I noticed the card. I instantly felt myself flush. He not only worked for the FBI himself, but he was the Special Agent in Charge (SAC) of the Pittsburgh Division. When I looked up to see him smiling at me from across the room, I mouthed the words, "I'm sorry."

At the end of the day, the gentleman reapproached me and we spent a few minutes discussing our mutual careers. It wasn't too long before he broached the subject of an employment opportunity with the Bureau. I was thrilled at the prospect. He invited me to meet with him at his office, and I happily agreed. A few weeks later, we met and he convinced me to apply for the Community Outreach Specialist position. After careful thought about the pros and cons, I applied and went through the hiring process. When the interviews and background investigation were completed, I finished as the top candidate and was offered the job. The following January, I joined the ranks of the Federal Bureau of Investigation (FBI), Pittsburgh Division. In doing so, I was able to fulfill one of my childhood dreams.

Now, the position sounds glamorous, but I would be lying if I said that job was easier than working for the police department. In some ways, it was even harder and I found adjusting to my new responsibilities just as difficult as the early days of my policing career. The bureaucracy of the federal government agency was quite stifling and some of the men seemed to think we were still in the days of J. Edgar Hoover. However, within the agency, I also found some of the most dedicated men and women that I had ever had the privilege of serving with. Each of these wonderful individuals brought a special skill to their métier.

They were highly educated, trained, and consummate professionals who dove into their work and assignments. I found a comfort in knowing that such individuals of high integrity were working for the Bureau.

In the early months of my employment, I found it somewhat hard to fit in and never quite found my comfort zone. But I was grateful for the opportunity and took great satisfaction from working within and for the community. After the events of 9/11, the difficult internal turmoil I felt intensified as our responsibilities increased. With the added duties of safeguarding the country from any future terrorist attacks, the office environment became even more "dog-eat-dog." Most of the employees worked feverishly to help ensure 9/11 would never happen again. The result was that the Bureau became a very stressful place to work. With each passing day spent at a breakneck pace, my mind delved into a state of high anxiety.

As my mind edged further away from the stress of the office, I found my home away from home with the Division's external partners. I flourished on the outside in collaborating with them on innumerable endeavors, and I forged partnerships with some of the most amazing individuals walking this earth. Over an extended time period, we were able to develop some significant youth violence prevention and reduction initiatives that achieved outstanding outcomes. Of this time in my career, I am the most proud. Working with such service-minded individuals made me feel that I had truly answered my call to service. I had done as God had asked me to do: I had accepted a mission to protect and serve in the best interest of all children.

But this chapter of my life did not end as happily as it had started. As a result of my service at the Flight 93 crash site in Shanksville, Pennsylvania, on September 11, 2001, I was diagnosed with post-traumatic stress disorder (PTSD). Ultimately, I was deemed medically unable to perform my duties. The horrific events and their aftermath had traumatized my mind. In the years following 9/11, symptoms and behaviors associated with PTSD became imbedded in my being. I suffered from anxiety, depression, fatigue, fibromyalgia, flashbacks, headaches, heart arrhythmia, rhinitis, startle effect, and stomach ailments. Despite any efforts to heal, I was unable to find any relief. I entered into one of the most troubling times of my life. As I attempted to recuperate at home, another event caused further damage to my already troubled psyche, and my world as I knew it was dramatically altered.

It all began with a knock at my front door. After peering through my living room window to determine the identity of the unannounced visitor, I glanced at the street and noticed a dark-colored vehicle parked directly across from my home. As soon as I saw the car, I immediately knew whoever was waiting for me to open the door was an employee of the federal government. After you have worked for the FBI, you can identify the vehicles driven by other members of the agencies quite easily. Although the cars are meant to be nondescript to some degree, they are unmistakable if you know what to look for: they have antennas and other markings that set them apart, not to mention an ominous energy. When I opened my door to greet the strange man standing on my front porch, he proceeded to flash his badge and identify himself as an agent with the Office of Inspector General (OIG). He handed me a document, which he proceeded to explain was a grand jury subpoena.

I was rendered speechless. I could not fathom what I could have possibly done to bring a representative of the

OIG to my door. The agency only conducted investigations when there was an allegation of misconduct or criminal activity. In my mind, this agent surely had made a mistake.

Before he began to speak, his demeanor told me everything I needed to know. After all, he was an interrogator and trained to intimidate by his mere presence. In the short time he was in my house, it was apparent he was conducting an initial interview. When I was finally able to speak, I asked a few questions. He responded to them in a less-than-cordial manner. The tone of his voice made it all too evident that he was already convinced I had committed some crime.

When the man left my home, I fell to my knees and prayed for divine guidance. Once again, in that time of need, I heard the Archangel Michael whisper in my ear.

"All is well. You are not a victim. You are a victor. In time, all shall be revealed."

When the Archangel finished speaking, I felt his warmth encompass me. And for the first time since I answered that knock at my front door, a peace came over me.

In the days following the OIG agent's visit, I was heartbroken and in disbelief over the situation. In my mind, I had lost the precious reputation I had promised Dad I would protect. And my psyche was crushed by the way that some people turned their backs on me, especially my colleagues at the Bureau. But as my despair grew, so did my faith in God. I firmly believed God knew the truth. I felt the Lord would extend His hand and send Archangel Michael to draw his sword and cut away the cords that bound me to these lies.

Over the next eight months, I waited for the investigation to take its course. As each day passed, I received telephone calls from acquaintances and former colleagues to let me know they had been visited by OIG agents. With every conversation, they reassured me that there was nothing for me to worry about. Each individual believed that, based on the type of questions asked, the allegations were unfounded. When finally the day arrived for me to be interviewed, I was told by the investigators that they had found no evidence of any criminal activity. Hearing those words brought me great relief, but I felt a deep anger and resentment toward those who had been a part of the probe. How dare they question my integrity! I had been a loyal employee and had worked long hours to help the Bureau achieve its mission.

It would take some time for me to come to terms with all that had transpired. And in the months that followed, I realized my anger had resulted from a personal crisis of identity. For 25 years, my identity revolved around my job. I lived and breathed law enforcement, and its procedures were deeply ingrained in me. I had dedicated myself to serving the greater good for all humanity. However, what I came to learn was that this self was not who I truly was; it was merely one dimension of my entity. Under the guise of my law enforcement persona, I had the opportunity to study my fellow man. It gave me the chance to learn about human behavior and to restore some order to an otherwise chaotic world. The job, however, allowed for me to fulfill only a portion of my life's purpose. As this insight came to me, I began to regain a sense of self-worth. Over time, my self-esteem was restored. In the bittersweet surrendering of my career at the FBI, I had opened a channel to let my inner voice find its way to be heard again.

In time, I became increasingly aware that the drama of the investigation had lost its hold on me. My ego quieted down, and my identity evolved. As the vile, muddy waters of this chapter of my life cleared, I found my way again by following my soul toward grace. Just like a young seedling breaking its way to the top of the soil, I was slowly rising out of the depths of the dirt piled on top of me with a new identity, a healthier energy, and vitality for life. My perception of the events changed as I contemplated them. As my awareness shifted, so did my priorities. I was able to see past the convoluted messages I was receiving about my identity, and to clarify for myself what I wanted that to be. The dark and negative energy that had surrounded me for far too long turned into energy expressed in tones of lovely, soft hues of color. I was reinvigorated at all of the prospects of what was yet to be.

As I reflected on my spiritual growth, I realized that a few amazing events had also recently come to pass during this time in my life. For one, Vanessa learned to see me in a different light. She saw her once strong and stoic mother evolve into a softer, more vulnerable creature. Family members with whom I had severed ties showed up to lend their support. And old friends from my early days of policing offered a shoulder for me to cry on. So despite the pain caused by a blow that had come so unexpectedly, those marvelous gifts kept me from feeling completely downtrodden. I had apparently learned how to find the good in any bad situation. My glass, to some, may have appeared half empty, but in my heart, it was half full.

In times of weakness, I have dropped to my knees and implored God for His help. This time, I had heard the whispers echo in my ear: "When prayers go up, blessings come down." That moment of lucidity helped me find my authentic identity. My spirit cried out in joy: "I am a child of the Most High God. I am a mirror image of His love and light. I am worthy of only good to come into my life."

In the months that followed my discharge from duty, I slowly found my path toward healing and spiritual enlightenment. With each day and each step, I drew closer to acquiring the knowledge, skills, and abilities to adapt to a new life and to acknowledge the rapture of my soul.

In the years following my diagnosis of PTSD, I sought healing from a myriad of doctors, medications, and integrative therapies. But none of those abated my symptoms. That is, not until I began Eye Movement Desensitization Reprocessing (EMDR) therapy with a highly skilled psychologist who was able to guide me toward healing. As I journeyed on a path to restore my health, I began to journal my thoughts and emotions. Over time, journaling became one of my most effective treatments. With each page I penned, I seemed to be able to rid myself of some of the anxiety and depression that plagued me. When I discovered that the journal had transformed into something more, a book, I sought avenues for publishing my rendition of the events of September 11, 2001, and its aftermath. In writing my first book, *In the Shadow of a Badge*, I came to better understand the journey that began on that fateful day. It was one of the worst days in American history, but the events that transpired led to my own spiritual awakening. My hope is that, by sharing the chapters of my life here, others may relate to my journey and find their own paths to healing their bodies, minds, and spirits.

CHAPTER 26

THE RETURN
OF A BROTHER

As I journeyed to heal from the effects of the PTSD, I was required to do a personal review of my life and identify any significant events that could have caused me to create a tough facade. Although I knew that somewhere deep inside me dwelled an open heart, life had persuaded me to close it as the good, the bad, and the ugly circumstances occurred. These instructional pieces, as I came to refer to them, resulted from situations that caused a great deal of pain and sorrow—not only for me, but for the other individuals involved. It took years, though, for me to see how the outcomes of those events allowed me to find redemption. The last few chapters of this book relate special moments in my life when "aha" triumphs finally arrived.

In the weeks immediately following the launch of the OIG investigation, the stress of the legal issues became almost unbearable for me. I knew myself to be innocent of their allegations. And yet, my mind was tortured by the notoriety and gossip a single newspaper article about it had caused. My nights were sleepless and my days were riddled with anxiety over the mounting pressure I felt. I experienced an ever-increasing escalation of anger, disbelief, and disappointment in the agency that I had served. The investigation reminded me in the most painful way that not all men—or women, for that matter—are interested in serving the greater good. During my days wearing the blue, I had come across individuals all too frequently who walked the earth taking great pleasure from causing rancor in another's life.

I awoke one Saturday morning feeling particularly abandoned and let down. As my emotions reached their peak of despair, I heard a knock at my front door and glanced out the window to determine who it might be. To my surprise, there standing on my porch was one of my brothers. I was stunned to see him because we had not shared a close relationship for quite some time. I opened the door somewhat hesitantly at first, thinking perhaps he had come to chastise me.

"Sis, are you all right?" he asked.

As soon as he said those words, I shook my head and began to cry. That moment of painful expression brought me some comfort, though, as my brother opened his arms and wrapped them around me. At his gesture of kindness, I let my head fall on his shoulder. I sobbed. As he tightened his arms around me, I felt as if I had been enfolded into the arms of my beloved Archangel Michael. It was as though every inch of his magnificent wings was cradling my troubled being, and I felt a similar surrounding warmth. I knew Archangel Michael had sent my brother as a messenger. As the recognition of that became clear, I knew our deceased father must have had a hand in sending my brother as well.

We stood in the foyer of my home for a few minutes before moving into the kitchen. As my brother sat down on the chair, he asked, "What can I do for you, sis?"

I smiled through my reddened and swollen eyes. "You've already helped me by being here. You must have been sent by Archangel Michael to watch over me."

He laughed and proceeded to remind me that his Confirmation name was Michael and that guardian angels could take many forms. He then explained that he had heard a voice softly whisper to him. The voice said that he should come see me. I smiled in complete understanding, because in my heart I knew that it was Archangel Michael who had spoken to my brother.

We sat for a time and talked. He shared the latest news about his life. He also expressed his concerns about my situation. I reassured him I would be all right. I explained that although I felt stressed and fragmented, I somehow knew I would be able to sustain myself until the circumstances improved.

When my brother got up to leave, I was sad to see him go. In visiting, he had brought the comfort I had sorely needed. And for a brief time, it had felt as if Dad were with us in the room. As he walked out, he shared some words of wisdom.

"Sis, don't let this situation make you lose your faith," he said.

When he finished speaking, my eyes again filled with tears. "My faith has only grown stronger. God knows the truth, and He will bring about a peaceful resolution to this matter."

In a quiet moment of reflection later that evening, I thought about how there is no perfect human being or ideal relationship—especially when it comes to families and, in particular, siblings. Each of us is imperfect in our design. This must have been God's plan, and His way of helping us all become better individuals. Our relationships and our choices help us grow. And even though we all have our imperfections, on occasion we all get to experience perfect love in our hearts. My handsome brother was a reflection of this perfect love. Out of this negative situation arose the opportunity for us to reconnect. In my moment of pain, he reached inside his heart and extended kindness through his strong and comforting arms. A single moment clarified for me his place in my life, and helped me on my path to healing.

His visit helped me remember a childhood incident. I had fallen off a swing, and as I lay there crying on the ground, he had picked me up in his arms and carried me to the safety of the porch. Almost immediately, I had felt secure again. I was grateful for his presence then, and I was thankful for his presence that morning as well. It brought me great solace and helped me reconnect my heart and soul.

CHAPTER 27

VALENTINES
FOR WHOOLEY

In the months that followed my medical leave from the Bureau, my mind drifted even deeper into the throes of depression. My once-vibrant and alert mind seemed to be able to dwell only on the negative facets of my life. It felt as if all the joy had been sucked right from my very core. As the darkness of the days seeped into my mind, I heard some news that further disheartened my spirit. The news came in the most unconventional of ways. One April morning, I was awakened by the sound of my telephone ringing. As my mind tried to focus and become oriented to my surroundings, I reached for the phone. When I answered it in my confused state, I heard the voice of a dear friend and mentor on the other end of the line. I could tell she was eager to speak with me because her voice had an urgent tone to it. I became worried, thinking that something was wrong with her or her husband. Before I could utter a word, she stated that she had an important message for me. Without any further hesitation, she said that during the early hours of the morning, as she lay in her bed, she had been visited by my deceased father's spirit. I listened intently as she told me what Dad had said: "Tell

Lillie it is my time to leave now. She doesn't need me any longer. She is stronger than she thinks. She is like an oak tree and can now stand on her own. Tell her all is well. I go now to prepare for the others who are yet to come."

As she finished her words, I began to sob. Since Dad's death, I had indeed felt his spirit present. And at every crossroad, I felt his guidance, too. He had found a way to remain in my life and to continue to counsel me. As my memories of Dad filtered through my mind in a quick and brilliant succession, I told my friend that I fully believed all she had shared. She is an intuitive with a great gift of sight, and she had relayed messages to me about my life many times before. I had also found her to be highly skilled at channeling the spirit world. I thanked her for her willingness to share what she had heard.

When our conversation ended, I felt compelled to go and visit my father's grave site. I drove in the pouring rain to the cemetery. While standing next to his headstone, I reached down and touched the imprint of his name, which had been intricately etched. I tried to visualize him in my mind as he had been before the cancer drained him of his once mighty stance. I saw him as he looked in many of the photos hanging in my home, photographs that recorded his life from his earliest days as a toddler to just weeks before he died. As I stood there in the rain, I felt a kindred bond with the sky because, like the rain clouds I, too, was releasing tears on his grave. As my tears and the raindrops mingled as one, I uttered my good-byes to Dad, just as I had done some 15 years earlier when he was first laid to rest. But this time, my farewell was of a different nature. I truly had to let him go to his place of rest. When I finally left the cemetery, I did so with a deep sadness weighing heavy on my heart.

Later that day, I went downstairs into my basement to place some documents into a small metal filing cabinet. When I opened the drawer, I noticed a couple of files that were labeled "Personal Info." It had been awhile since I had looked through the numerous files hidden away in that cabinet drawer. I opened one and saw that it contained cards Dad had sent to me over the years, mostly birthday and Valentine's Day cards. When I touched the cards, my mind flashed back to the precious moments in life when I had been lucky enough to receive them from Dad. He was such a sentimental man. I vividly recalled the mornings that I would awaken to find a card on the pillow of my bed, waiting for me to open it.

As I lifted out a tiny white envelope, I began to cry all at once. When I was little, I wasn't able to pronounce "Lillie," so instead I would say "Whooley," and that had been one of Dad's nicknames for me—and that was how he had addressed the card. Dad often called me that when he wanted to express some affection or poke some fun at me. As I touched each of the cards, I traced the words he had written and his signed name as well. Each time I ran my fingers across his signature, I noticed how warm my hand felt. But the heat of my hand paled in comparison to the warmth in my heart. My eyes welled with tears again, because I felt overcome by gratitude for having had such a man in my life. I stopped reminiscing for a moment and quietly offered a prayer. I thanked God for my dad and for reminding me of how well I was loved. I thought about how love transcends all time and space. Love is sustained in memories from our lives. In that moment of fond remembrance, I had a powerful realization: Dad would never really be gone. He would always remain a part of me, even if he was now far beyond the limits of his human life.

His soul was connected to mine, as it was to Mom's, my siblings', my daughter's, and his mother's, too. As I placed that card back into its envelope, I felt the corners of my mouth curl into a smile. And as I wiped the last of my tears away, I prayed that Dad's eternal soul would find repose in the House of Elohim.

CHAPTER 28

THE BEST
CATCH EVER

"Get out of your head and back to your heart," an old friend whispered to me one day as we were walking around a local track. As I pondered her comment, I realized she was right. For all too long, I had lived in a state of mind-straining study and I had repressed my nurturing capabilities for the benefit of my analytical and stressful law enforcement career. I was constantly surrounded by negative energy, and I was always caught up in the many anxiety-inducing situations and events my professional life presented. As a result, I failed to notice that my heart had become closed. Or that my spirit was tired. And as my mind became sharper at work, my authentic self kept fading into the distance. As I edged ever closer to a permanent lack of heartfelt contentment, my friend's simple words awakened my spirit again. I realized that it was time to create some space in my life for the positive.

I had waited many years for the "right" life, the "right" person, and the "right" pathway to materialize. I held my breath in anticipation of all those things, forgetting to exhale. The lesson I have learned about waiting for something to happen is that you spend far too much time analyzing things. I forgot how to be spontaneous and joy-ful. In my youth, I had gone after what I wanted. My heart's desires raged through my body, and I relished each and every savory moment in pursuit of them. As I moved into adulthood, I pursued my goals with passion and met every challenge head-on. As I grew into middle age, though, I began to hesitate and suppress those urges and ignore my own needs. Somehow, somewhere along the way, my need to devour and be nourished by life had been curtailed and my appetite for exploration had diminished. I felt the light go out inside of me, but I had no idea how to rekindle the old, burning desires. I could not quite comprehend how to reignite my soul.

In the days leading up to my 53rd birthday, it was once again the time of the waxing moon. In the late eve-ning hours of that week, I would step outside to look at the beautiful oval-shaped moon brightly glowing in the sky as it grew into its own fullness. The contrast of dark blue clouds also helped the moon to shine ever clearer in the quiet stillness of the night. As I looked at the moon one evening, I decided to meditate and allow the positive energy from the atmosphere to flow through me. Over the past few days, I had felt closed off, but I knew the fresh air would restore me. As I closed my eyes and inhaled, I felt the cool, crisp air make its way through my throat, into my chest, and then into my lungs. With each breath, the cooling sensation helped to reinvigorate me. As my spirit began to lift out of its gloomy state, I prayed for a miracle to occur in my life. I longed for some peaceful resolution and a return of my former vibrant health as well. My mind swirled as I tried to release the tension of the past months, and I had a vision of the Archangel Haniel. I could see her so clearly in my mind's eye: a beautiful female spirit surrounded by soft blue and white hues.

As I felt her warm embrace encompass me, I remembered that the Archangel Haniel works her miracles in synchronicity with the moon's cycles. With the moonbeams streaming down above me, I stood there, alone in the darkness of my front yard, and implored the Archangel to help. As part of the invocation, I asked to be set free from past sorrows that were keeping me frozen in time and were not allowing anything new to flow into my life. I requested that the Archangel provide me with whatever insight would be necessary to break the bonds that tied me to the past. I begged to be released from all of the issues that burdened my soul, and asked for her guidance in directing my future path. As I stood there with the night sky wrapped around me, I felt my spirit stir. And once again, I heard the soft whispers in my ear. This whispering voice was not one that I had heard before. It was softer, more feminine in tone. I felt instantly comforted. Her message relayed that my prayers had been heard and that my wish would come true on my birthday. I closed my eyes once more and prayed for the winds of change to arrive in my life.

Just a couple of days later, I received a nice surprise as part of my birthday celebration. Michael came calling. The opportunity to visit with him again was as pleasant as it was unexpected. His visit ultimately helped him release pain. We fell quickly into our usual pattern of spending some time talking about our lives. As our conversation turned to the topic of our families, I felt compelled to ask Michael a strange question.

"What would you say to my dad if he were alive today?" I asked. "What would you want him to know about our relationship?"

Michael smiled that old familiar grin and responded without any hesitation, "I would tell your dad you were the best catch I ever made."

His eyes filled with tears, and I could tell by the look on his face that his mind had gone back to his football-playing days. For a moment, he became the running back scurrying down the field with a ball firmly held in his hands again. And as he relived those memories so dear to his heart, I knew he was filled with a sense of pride in his accomplishments. This man, who had a tough time putting his feelings into words, had just touched my heart by comparing me to the sport—and the life—that he had once treasured. I wondered whether he wanted to rekindle our relationship. Was it time for us to walk across the line of scrimmage hand in hand and find out once and for all if we had what it took to win at the game of love?

As I sat looking across the kitchen table at that complicated man, I felt a new sense of admiration for him. In that moment, I realized if Dad had still been alive for the past few years, maybe he and Michael would have had an opportunity to discuss our situation. Maybe Dad would have been able to look past Michael's character flaws and accept his lovely spirit within. As I thought about Michael's words, I realized some of the problem may have been the fact that these two men were more alike than either cared to admit. They were both very masculine and strong, and each was used to being the alpha male and very much in control. Both were also deeply spiritual and athletically inclined. No matter what the problem, Dad and Michael could draw a parallel, a parable, or a solution from either the Bible or football.

That evening, Michael and I entered into a new state of awareness about our connection. A divine intervention took place that helped us reach our joint revelation. All good things do indeed come in time—they just don't necessarily happen in our time, but in God's time. It had taken all too many years for Michael and me to get to that place. As we stood there embracing in my kitchen, I knew this chapter in our lives would offer some form of mutual healing. It was now time for us to emerge from our past and find out if we had what it took to be together. Were we destined to be a championship team, or were we destined to remain merely former teammates who felt a bond of great camaraderie but nothing more? As I pondered these thoughts, I was comforted by the fact that the answers would soon be revealed one way or another.

A few months passed before Michael paid another visit. And as was his usual style, he arrived unannounced at my doorstep again. There had been spans when I did not see him for months or years at a time. Despite promises to alter his ways, his intermittent visits came at times of his choosing and without any courtesy call or forewarning. I believed this cavalier behavior to be one of his biggest character flaws, and was one of the reasons I doubted his ability to commit to a permanent relationship.

Michael explained that he was in town to celebrate Labor Day weekend. His family would be gathering at his mother's home for their annual barbecue and, to my surprise, he had asked if I might want to accompany him. At first, I was somewhat apprehensive about going. I had never participated in any of his family's events. I thought it might be a bad idea.

But as I opened my mouth and began to decline his invitation, Michael stopped me. "You have to stop being so guarded with people. It's time for you to come out of your shell and find the happiness in your life."

At first, his words startled me. But, as I opened my mouth to object to what he had said, I felt an unseen hand nudge me forward and whisper in my ear, "Give his comments some careful consideration."

Once again, Archangel Michael was encouraging me to listen to his namesake. I stood there for a moment in silence while I considered the invitation. Meeting his family would be an important next step in our relationship. I believed it was truly time to find out where our path might lead, so I accepted.

As we drove to his mother's home that evening, we mostly made small talk. I tried to concentrate on what he was saying, but my mind was fixated on the moment when I would walk into his mother's home. Before I knew it, Michael was parking his car in front of the house. He turned to look at me, and he must have sensed my nervousness.

"Are you all right?" he asked.

I shook my head in a negative manner. I found it hard to speak because I could feel emotion rising in my throat. The expression of fear on my face answered his question. In an attempt to soothe me, Michael reached across and took my hand in his.

He said, "What are you worried about? Don't you know we are finally free? There is no one to stand in our way anymore. There is no husband, no wife, no boyfriend or girlfriend to hurt. There are no small children to worry about. They are all grown and living their own lives. There is no law enforcement agency dictating what you can and cannot do. For the first time since we met, it is just you and me, Lil. We are free at last to do what we want with the rest of our lives. If we choose to be a couple, it's our decision. If we choose to stay just close friends, it's our choice to make. It's all up to us. How does that make you feel?"

I felt the tears well up in my eyes. When I opened my mouth to reply, I found it hard to express the emotions that were rushing through my mind. His empathy for me gave rise to a new dimension of admiration for him. He understood me, and he truly knew how to guide and comfort me in the most trying times of my life.

I smiled and squeezed Michael's hand in mine. "It is good to know this part of our lives is just for us."

When I finished, I felt something stir deep inside. I wondered what was happening. Then I suddenly remembered what my friend had said about getting out of my mind and back to the inner workings of my heart. I fought the urge to analyze the moment, and inwardly smiled at her wise words. Now I finally comprehended what she had really meant: I needed to stop questioning every emotion and to start allowing myself to feel and to laugh again. Joy would help me open my heart.

As we walked up the stairs to his mom's front porch, I felt elated at the prospect of rebirth in this midlife moment of our journey. Each step we took became symbolic of the future steps that were waiting for us. As his hand tightly grasped mine, he opened the front door and we strolled into the house together. As soon as I began greeting his family members, I felt the anxiety drain from my body and a quiet contentment take hold.

Later that evening, I went outside to once again gaze at the moon. As on past nights, I felt the moon's energy mingle with mine. For a moment, I just stood there and allowed the energy to wash over me. It felt good to be in the place I had now ventured. I wanted to relish the present and give thanks for all that had come to pass. I bowed my head in prayer and expressed my gratitude to the Lord. As I stood there in the moonlight, I was once again reminded of how recent events had unfolded on a divine timeline, not on a human-directed one. And in that quiet moment, standing there under the stars, I heard a voice softly whisper, "All good things come in God's time."

On hearing those words of wisdom, I smiled. "Okay, God," I said. "I understand."

As I walked back into my home and closed the front door, I rejoiced with a song of rebirth. It was time to quit waiting for all of the "right" moments and things to come my way. It was time to break free of my restraints, to explore, and to feast on life again. My soul began to dance again in a harmonious rhythm with my heart. It was as if my entire being was finally engaged in a waltz and I swayed to its rhythm and melody. My mind then fluttered over and joined in harmony with the rest of me. It was then and only then that I caught myself making what I thought must be a glimmer of a smile. Was it finally happiness? I pondered that question. Was it peeking around the corner and about to turn my life in favor of effervescence and a new beginning? Only time would be able to write the next chapter and the true ending of this affair of the heart.

CHAPTER 29

THE LAKE HOUSE

As I mentioned before, I have always been drawn to water, especially the ocean. There, by the surf and sand, my spirit is uplifted and my mind is at ease. I seem to breathe a bit slower, speak in gentler tones, and sleep longer hours. I am rejuvenated by the sounds and smells of the sea. It is here of all places that I sense the presence of God. Although I prefer the wide expanse of the sea, I have found solace in visiting lakes, too. When I am near wildlife and rhythmic waves, I know I will be able to replenish my weary mind and tired body.

In the months that followed my medical discharge from the FBI, I made a new friend named Judy. We met at a dinner party hosted by a mutual friend who was kind enough to introduce us. As the evening progressed, Judy and I found we had much in common and our experiences made us feel somehow connected. We discussed how we were both in states of transition. Before I left the party that night, Judy invited me to visit her and her husband at their home on Lake Norman, in North Carolina. So when summer arrived that year, I made my first trek to the lake.

When I arrived at Judy's home, her warm hospitality felt like a welcome harbor from the storms of life. The house was very large, and she offered me my own private quarters. There, in the quiet, spacious lodgings, I could look out the windows and admire the beauty of the lake. The residence was in close proximity to a bird sanctuary, so I was also able to observe many different species of wildlife. Almost every morning, I saw blue herons, white cranes, geese, and hawks all gliding across the sky. The soaring birds reminded me of how important it was to let go and feel the brilliance of just being alive. The lake waters provided a healing energy, and the burdens and trials and tribulations that had traveled with me began to ease away. Soon, I found myself more relaxed than I had been in recent months. It seemed each movement of the waves helped me release the stresses that plagued me. Before too long, my heart and mind were moving with the rhythm of each cresting ripple. Over the next week, I spent a great deal of time basking in the sun and allowing its warmth to revitalize my being. With each passing day, I felt balance returning to my spirit. It was a time of renewal, and I luxuriated in the serenity of Judy's lakeside oasis. My senses gradually reawakened and I began to see, hear, and feel the presence of an ever-increasing energy stirring inside of me.

On the last morning of my stay, Judy and I were quietly chatting in the kitchen. As she shared some of her own problems with me, I sensed the deep emotional pain she was experiencing. In that moment, I felt such empathy for her and her plight. I found myself saying a silent prayer for the angels to intercede on her behalf. I then felt a strong sensation of warmth encompass me. A beautiful shade of aquamarine-hued light enshrouded both Judy and me. As the warm feeling permeated my entire being, my arms spontaneously moved up from my torso in an arched motion, as if I was extending them to take flight. All at once, my hands moved upward to gently cradle Judy's face.

I heard the whispers inside my ear again, and I shared the words being uttered with her. Although I was physically present in the kitchen, I felt another presence take hold of me. For a period of a few minutes, I seemed to lose my sense of time and space; I experienced only the fieriness and the brilliant aura of pure light.

When I again became aware of my surroundings, I felt disoriented. It took me a few moments to regain my senses. When I did, I noticed Judy had tears in her eyes and that she appeared quite shaken. Without my speaking a word, Judy told me that she had just had an angelic encounter. As she described her experience, I knew it had to be true. She said the angel had delivered a message of comfort and reassurance. Although I was not cognizant of all that Judy had experienced, I did recall hearing the name Raguel. Judy then shared that the angel had introduced himself as Archangel Raguel.

I was speechless. I quickly left the kitchen and retreated to the shelter of my guest quarters. There, in the quiet of the sunlit room, I stared out at the lake. As I tried to digest all that had occurred, I asked God for answers. Had another archangel manifested? But how? Why? The experience as Judy related it seemed too far-fetched for me to grasp fully. I prayed and listened, but heard no whispers. When I returned to the kitchen, I did my best to avoid any further discussion with Judy about the encounter. As I said my good-byes and drove away from the lake, I still felt dazed by the morning's events.

A few days after that experience, I still felt very confused by the angelic apparition. I began to scour through all the reference books in my small library, searching for clues that might help answer the questions that were swirling in my mind. As I perused the pages of several books,

I came upon a passage about Archangel Raguel. It read: "Archangel Raguel's name means 'friend of God.' His role is to serve as an intermediary between God and humanity. His forte is bringing harmony to both personal and professional relationships. He is a wonderful resolver of conflicts and helps to defend those unfairly treated. When Raguel manifests, he is known to be enshrouded by a pale blue aura."

After reading through those pages, some answers dawned on me. The Archangel Raguel had arrived to ease Judy's troubled mind. In doing so, he had comforted her and relieved her fear about a situation that was causing her great despair. Perhaps he had also arrived to identify himself as her guardian angel as well, I thought. I felt relieved to know that the Archangel was present and would keep Judy safe from harm. I knew from my own experience of being blessed by the presence of the Archangel Michael that with Archangel Raguel by her side, all would indeed be well. Through my Archangel's divine intervention, I had received much grace. And now it seemed that a good friend was embarking on her own spiritual quest. I hoped she would come to trust that her Archangel would serve in her best interest.

This lakeside encounter with the angels was the first of a series for me. It was the dawn of my enhanced connection with angelic beings and the further evolution of my spiritual life.

CHAPTER 30

LET THERE BE PEACE

As I progressed on my path of healing, I experienced the highs and lows that come with depression. On more days than I care to admit, I found myself wallowing in self-pity and immobilized by fear. On one particular morning, the anxiety and chronic pain were uncontrollable and I was having a tough time coping. As I showered that morning, I found myself singing an old hymn that I had learned when I attended church as a child: "Let There Be Peace on Earth." It is still one of my favorites. When I began to sing, I felt my tension dissipate. But as I belted it out, I was thankful no one else could hear me. I didn't have much of a voice to begin with, and the laryngitis I was suffering from at the time further affected my vocal cords. My singing probably sounded more like a wounded animal's howl than a joyful melody. Despite my limited capabilities as a songstress, I felt the words of the hymn resonate with me and a sense of solace take hold.

A few minutes after showering, I happened to look outside my kitchen window. There, perched on the telephone wires hanging above my home, was a mourning dove. The bird was pale gray in color and it had a long neck. It sat quietly on the wire and it was looking up at the sky. I smiled when I saw the bird. Long ago, Situ had told me, "When you see a dove, you'll know it is me."

So as I looked at the tiny creature, I smiled at the memory of her love. I felt a warmth take hold of me, and my smile broadened across my face. Within seconds, two more doves arrived, and then, after a few more seconds, *another* two doves landed on the wire. As I looked at their delicate facial features, I again smiled at the prospect that my grandmother had brought some family members or perhaps some friends with her to help brighten my day.

As I watched the lovely winged creatures, I felt the essence of God stir in my soul. I knew He had sent me a sign—the dove is a symbol of the Holy Spirit and of peace. I realized I had just received another ounce of grace. I also reflected on how each time I had called to the Lord for some relief, He had responded. In that moment, I felt so blessed. It was comforting to know the lovely little birds had been sent to remind me all was well. I closed my eyes and gave thanks for the gift. When I opened them again, the birds were in the midst of flying away. And within seconds, the doves were gone from my sight. As the birds took flight, I realized my ill mood had gone with them. The burdens had been lifted, and I felt calm again.

After watching the doves fly away, I happened to look out a smaller window positioned on the other side of my kitchen. I could see a beautiful angel standing on the hillside directly behind my home. The angel had a male form, soft light brown hair, and he was illuminated by white light and soft hues of blue. Once again, I smiled. "Welcome," I said to the heavenly messenger.

As I spoke, more angels gathered and within seconds there were many celestial beings standing around the perimeter of my yard. They stood along the property line as if to form a spiritual fence that would guard against any enemies. Each of the angelic visitors was surrounded by a misty white light and a pale blue aura. As I looked at each of their faces, I was reminded of 9/11 and the field of angels I had witnessed at the Flight 93 crash site. The lovely winged messengers of light had provided such comfort on that fateful day. I wondered if they had returned now to bring comfort to my overly burdened heart, mind, and soul. They created a strong presence around my statue of the Blessed Mother sitting ever so still upon her small grotto of stone. As I looked across my yard, I was filled with gratitude for Mary and her legions of angels. They reminded me of God's universal love and His desire for peace in our chaotic world.

It was in that moment that I once again remembered we are never alone, and that God grants miracles. All you need do is believe, have faith, and trust in the Lord. As I ruminated on the higher power of God, the vision of the angels disappeared. They left behind such a strong feeling of grace that I felt somehow healed.

That day eventually turned to night, and I awoke from my sleep to see the most wondrous display of twinkling lights illuminating my room. Everywhere I looked, I saw an array of colors dancing across the walls and the ceiling. The dazzling spectrum of lights was in tones of sky blue, soft pink, and coral intermixed with ivory white. Each color was as brilliant and as lovely as the next, and it seemed like the lights were taking turns drawing my attention. As I watched the wondrous kaleidoscope of color moving before my eyes, I smiled; I knew the Archangels were close. The angelic beings had arrived again to remind me that all would be well. As I slipped back to sleep, I was comforted by the knowledge that the winged messengers were near. I knew I was protected and need not worry. It was obvious the peace I had so longed for had been bestowed by the Lord on this night of bedazzled wonder.

In the days that followed that glorious manifestation, I again heard the whispers of Archangel Michael. His message was one of great enlightenment: he told me that the angelic visitation showed the sacred circle of Archangels, and that they were ever present and ready to respond when called. When they appeared, they came to serve the greater good of all mankind, just like they had done on 9/11.

From that day forward, I would think about the vision of the sacred circle of the Archangels regularly. And once, on a quiet September morning, I heard them, too. It happened on the tenth anniversary of 9/11, while I was attending the dedication ceremony of the Flight 93 Memorial. As my daughter and I drove onto the land where the crash happened, I heard a distant chant. At first, it was faint. But the closer we drove toward the memorial, the clearer, louder, and more high-pitched the chanting became. It sounded like hundreds of voices were singing in unison. I stopped for a moment to marvel at its beauty. I raised my face toward the sky and felt the warmth of the sun transfer down. I closed my eyes in an attempt to memorize the sounds I was hearing. I felt as if my heart and mind had merged, and I believe that my soul was welcomed to join in their revelry.

In the years that followed, I have tried to replicate the sound of the Archangels' chant myself. I will often use it to open gatherings, inviting the angelic beings to the space. And although my musical skills are limited, people in attendance have mentioned that they have felt the room become very warm: a sign of the angels announcing their arrival. They gather with us to guide, protect, and heal in all things great and small.

CHAPTER 31

ANGEL BABY

As the years have passed by, my family has changed and grown in number. Vanessa married and had three more children. I now have three granddaughters and one grandson, whom we fondly call "little man." And they now refer to me as "Situ." In choosing to carry on using the traditional Arabic name for grandmother, I feel as if I am honoring the lovely woman who instructed me about both the physical and metaphysical worlds.

Each of Vanessa's children possesses an intuitive gift, and their warm hearts and open minds have allowed for them to connect easily with the angelic realm. The eldest of the four is blessed with clairvoyance—her ability to see things is uncanny. The second child is very creative and an artist at heart. She is able to interpret the world in colorful designs. The third child appears to have various capabilities. She both hears and sees the angels and enjoys sharing her experiences with them. In addition, she developed a fondness for crystals at the tender age of nine months. The youngest seems to sense the angels' presence as well. On occasion he, too, has indicated that he has observed a visitation.

One cloudy afternoon, as I sat in the living room with my two younger granddaughters watching a movie, an angelic encounter took place. We sat there, simply engaging in our usual banter and sharing laughter and conversation about the movie. The moment was filled with contentment, and it etched itself forever in my memory banks. At one point, my granddaughters mentioned that the room seemed to feel very warm. I, too, noticed the temperature change, but I blamed it on the heat of the day and the air conditioner overworking itself. We turned our attention back to the television screen. Then, without warning, the electronic toys in the living room suddenly turned on and began to make noise. In fact, the gadgets seemed to be taking turns speaking and playing. It reminded me of the scene in the film *Close Encounters of the Third Kind* where the aliens attempted to communicate with the humans through a series of musical tones. The sounds the toys were making were eerily similar. As I got up to take a look around the room, I could feel the presence of an unseen visitor who had arrived, but who had not yet fully manifested.

When the noise finally stopped, all three of us turned to look at one another. The wide-eyed stares of the children said all that needed to be said. The eldest was the first to speak.

"What just happened, Situ?"

Before I could respond, the younger girl chirped, "Was someone playing with our toys?"

I smiled at both their questions. "It must be the angels visiting," I said. "Sometimes, when you can't see or hear them, they play with the electronics in the room. That way, you know they are present."

This answer seemed to calm the girls down, and we decided to continue watching the movie. Within a few minutes' time, though, the toys began to play once again.

Their sounds echoed across the room, and they seemed to reach a higher pitch than before. We looked at one another in wide-eyed wonder again. We were bewildered by the events taking place in the otherwise still house. This time, it was the younger granddaughter who first made a comment.

"Look, it's an angel," she said, pointing to the hallway. "It's a baby angel. She's a little girl with brown hair and wings. She is all dressed in white."

As I watched her begin to smile, I realized she had truly glimpsed the ethereal world. For a brief moment, it had merged with the earthly plane and my grandchild had seen into the angelic realm. I was so overjoyed. The look on the little one's face was one of pure delight. She was bedazzled by the splendor of what she had witnessed. She had been blessed with a visit from her guardian angel. I smiled at her and lifted her in my arms.

"Your angel wanted you to know she was here watching over you, the family, and the house, too," I softly whispered in her ear.

Although both granddaughters appeared to be lost in their own thoughts, they managed a half-smile for me. The older of the two shared that she had not seen the angel, but that she had felt its warmth.

"Someday you, too, will see the angels," I assured her. "All you need to do is open your heart and remove the doubt from your mind. Hold on to your faith," I added, "and someday soon you, too, will be able to communicate with God's messengers."

In the days that followed, I was informed that the children's toys continued to make noise on their own. So frequently, in fact, that Vanessa asked what I had done to make that phenomenon occur. In response, I merely smiled.

When I look back on this event, I do so with great happiness. Just like the generations before me who had the gift to feel, hear, and see these visitors, this next generation had it, too. My grandmother had taught me to open up to this special world and to be receptive to my intuitive gifts. Although Situ's devout Catholic upbringing seemed to restrict her from truly accepting her gift, she nevertheless helped me initiate an understanding of my own.

I feel honored to be able to teach my grandchildren about their divine gifts, and I believe we can learn from each other as well. My hope is to help them become comfortable with their skills.

I believe that we all possess the ability to feel, hear, and see the presence of the angels God sends to intervene on His behalf. We are all connected to the higher power of God and His universal energy. The everyday stresses of life, though, cause some of us to close ourselves off, and our skills for detecting them diminish. Or perhaps the childlike wonder of our youth simply slips away as we age and our busy lifestyles cause daily wear and tear on our spirits and drain us of our ability to stay connected to the celestial domain we once called home. But if we are willing to reconnect with the divine order of our souls, we can find magic everywhere.

In the coming years, I pray that I will witness many more visits from the angels. May these manifestations also become a part of the lives of my grandchildren and their grandchildren yet to be.

CHAPTER 32

THE LOST YEARS

Each time I thought I had finished writing this book, another chapter begged to be written. One such chapter related to my ex-husband and the emotions that had remained locked inside the chambers of my heart.

When I learned that he was critically ill, I was besieged by a flood of emotions that I was unaware had even existed. Although Vanessa and her dad had been estranged for a number of years, she became overwrought about his illness. Over the years, she had made repeated attempts to end their rift. However, despite all her efforts at reconciliation, they had never managed to fully resolve their differences. In talking with Vanessa about his current health condition, I reminded her that her father had once been capable of great love. In the very beginning of our life together, he had championed the right to be my husband and her father. In those early years of family life, he had been eager to express his emotions. But by the third year of our marriage, he had begun to abuse alcohol. When his alcoholism and violent outbursts got out of control, Vanessa and I had no choice but to pack up our belongings and leave. As I walked out the door that day, I believed I had left the pieces of a shattered marriage behind me.

In the years following my divorce, I convinced myself that I had rid myself of any feelings about my ex-husband

and the events that had transpired. Yet, when his health faltered, the leftover emotions long trapped inside my subconscious found the pathway to my conscious mind. And soon, I felt a convoluted mess of upheaval and regret surging inside my soul. His condition worsened with each passing day, and I was hit with emotions that I believed had long been gone.

As Vanessa and I spoke about her dad, I felt the remnants of old feelings stir. The dormant fragments of them had remained hidden for many years. During each conversation I tried to remain stoic as a means of easing her anxiety, but I could feel my own untapped emotions lying in wait within me. What I came to realize during that time was that I had developed an inability to ever make a true commitment to another man. For so many years, I needed closure. I suddenly felt a strong desire to speak with my ex and express these emotions. I became aware that the need was not only to resolve issues for me, but for Vanessa as well. The opportunity to do so would, I hoped, also help unlock closed chambers in my heart. I felt compelled to voice my feelings by talking with my ex before too much more time passed. I wanted to talk as a means of promoting healing for all three of us. I wanted him to know I forgave him for his indiscretions and ill behavior. And I hoped he would find it in his heart to forgive me for any trespasses I had committed against him as well. That first love we once shared had become a permanent part of my being. Years had swiftly passed, but I was still unable to truly accept another man's love. I sensed that my soul had not yet been released from the vow I had taken when we married.

When my ex-husband's health issues finally stabilized, I paid him a visit at his home. At first, we both seemed uncomfortable and lost in our own thoughts. When I began to speak about the present, though, the past hurts seemed to dissipate. I knew that nothing would be gained by rehashing the problems that had caused so much turmoil in our lives. Instead, I spoke to him about how much I appreciated that he had made an attempt to renew his relationship with our daughter. I also requested that he be very careful as to not injure her fragile heart again. Before I left, I asked if it would be all right to give him a hug. In his acceptance, I placed my arms around him and the emotions became somewhat overwhelming. For a moment, it felt as if the Archangel was present once again and that his strong and sturdy wings were enveloping us both. When finally I left that day, I felt so very relieved. All the stress and apprehension I had about making the visit faded away. In my heart, I believed we had come to a place of forgiveness in the arms of an angel.

Later that evening, as I sat contemplating all that had come to pass, I realized that my emotions were the result of grieving for the lost years. I was lamenting my inability to truly connect with or trust another man. I had closed myself off from all men, in a way, and hadn't allowed my heart to respond to the purity of new love. Although I had my share of romantic liaisons, I had closed my heart. I had built a great wall of protection around myself.

I've often asked myself why I stayed in a marriage that was obviously so destructive. It took me a very long time to answer this question, and I now understand that there were several reasons: I remained because of my religious upbringing, my embarrassment at being pregnant at a young age, and, most important, a deep-seated belief that I could "fix" my then-husband. Like other women who were taught to nurture everyone around them, I truly believed I was capable of this. I had to learn the hard way about loving and being loved. I finally realized that the problem lay in my inability to love myself. The simple act of self-love should come before anyone enters into any type of meaningful relationship. If I took the time to explore and truly understand myself before getting married, then, perhaps, I could have fully accepted love from a partner.

In the years that followed the dissolution of my marriage, I had to learn to forgive myself for past deeds. Part of that meant letting go of a belief system that no longer resonated with me. Not the conventional practice of devotion as it related to God, but the part of my organized religion that was meant to explain human behavior. I learned that my imperfections provided the most poignant lessons about becoming a better human being. I learned to identify these, and I now continually strive to correct negative behaviors that keep me from walking a spiritual path.

Now that I've worked to reconcile myself with my past, I feel an opening of my heart to the prospect of finding love again. I am vigilant about trying to recognize ongoing changes transpiring within me on a daily basis and how they affect my actions. I now understand I am an ever-evolving creature who has the ability to adapt to life's challenges. As I've aged, I've learned to shed some of my old skin and to change colors as needed in order to adapt to what life throws my way. My expectations of myself have changed, too. I am now more generous about my needs and more lenient on myself about my mistakes. I have entered a new dimension in a complex inner world, and my journey to that place shed light on the meaning of unconditional love. I feel blessed that God has provided me with Archangel Michael to help me move through all of these changes as I move forward on my personal quest.

CHAPTER 33

THE WISDOM
OF THE ELDERS

As I look back on my life, I am amazed at the twists and turns it has taken. In retrospect, I can see that it has been filled with times of pain and sorrow mixed with moments of sheer joy. Each chapter has moved my life toward surrender and grace. As a young child, I likened myself to a cat. Just like the lucky feline with its nine lives, I, too, had the ability to bounce back and survive. No matter what illness or negative event occurred, I somehow always landed on my feet. At first, I thought perhaps there were indeed nine lives locked inside my body. But as life marched on and the hands of the clock started to turn more quickly, it became apparent that my charmed life was due to more than sheer luck—it felt more designed. It took many years for me to fully understand that I had been blessed with God's grace.

A few months prior to the completion of this book, I was asked by one of my physicians about my chosen career. He queried, "If given the chance to go back in time, would you make the same choice about the law enforcement profession?"

Without hesitation I replied, "It was a great ride. I'd do it again in a heartbeat and recommend it to any younger woman considering law enforcement as a career."

As I smiled at him, I felt a sense of joy fill my mind, and my heart was consumed with a feeling of great pride. As I peered over the doctor's shoulder, I was sure I could see my grandmother Situ standing behind him and grinning. She seemed to be amused by our conversation. My mind slipped back in time to her eightieth birthday celebration and the question I had posed to her then. I asked her if she would go back in time if it meant she had the chance to be 30 years old again.

Situ responded, "Only if I could travel back with the wisdom it took me eighty years to acquire."

In that moment of reflection, I felt I finally understood my grandmother's prudent words. At the time, my younger mind couldn't grasp the full meaning of her words, but I now have clarity that only time can bestow, and my life has come full circle. My petite grandmother with the soft voice, lovely brown eyes, and brilliant smile had given me a wealth of knowledge to use in my future years. The elders in our lives can guide younger generations in valuable ways. They are the quintessential teachers about life and living because they have been through it. They are capable of providing priceless lessons, but we must learn to listen.

My own experience with the healing process reminds me that personal growth does indeed take time. I have even based my philosophy of life on a saying a friend once uttered to me: "Feel it, believe it, take action to achieve it, let go, and let God."

And I'll add one more element to that thought as well. We must learn to be patient with ourselves and with others. As I progressed with my own spiritual development,

I likened myself to a new seed planted in the ground. With careful cultivation, sunlight, water, fertilizer, and a prayer, it will grow into a healthy plant that is admired for its beauty. I have now realized that, although my outside beauty is fading with time, my inner glow is improving like a vintage wine. As a child, I was skinny, with big teeth and wild auburn hair, and I paled in comparison to the beauty of some other female members in the family. In addition, my tomboyish ways were not appreciated by some of my elders. As I recognized my lack of feminine beauty in the eyes of others, I once again turned to my dad for some guidance. As tears flowed down my face, he wiped them away and said, "Don't worry, little girl, because when God looks down from Heaven, He doesn't see the outside, He sees the beauty on the inside of your soul. So concentrate on your heart and spirit to make them shine."

When Dad told me that, I felt the truth of his words stir inside my soul—and that statement has remained with me to this day. I now embrace the gifts of knowledge my elders have shared with me, and also an ability to learn from life and to live each day as if it were my last. As the beauty of youth leaves my face and body, I know that it is not a reflection of the radiance of my soul. And when my final day on this earth arrives, I only hope I will see all the familiar faces of those who have left before me in the room. My wish is that God will bestow His grace one last time as His winged messengers carry me home.

CHAPTER 34

A SEASON OF EASE

Just like the changing seasons are marked by familiar characteristics, I can now look back and see that my life has had seasons, too. Each provided an opportunity for me to grow, though I didn't always recognize that at the time. I can now say that I have entered into a new season, a season of ease. I have become fully anointed in the knowledge of myself, but it took living through different experiences to get to this place of peace and revelation.

I had my winter with my sullen and isolated moods. I went dormant for a time, and had no real growth to speak of. As blustery winds howled and snow blew across the barren wasteland of the landscape, my soul felt similarly blanketed and held captive for a while. I was frozen in grief.

I had a fall season as well. When the leaves fell from the trees, so did the pieces of my broken heart fall away. With each brilliant, colorful leaf that danced in the wind, I felt as if my pain began to flutter away and release its strong hold on my mind as well.

I've had my spring in this life, too, with intermittent periods of new growth. My newly formed delicate petals made their way above the ground to peek through the soil into the sun. On occasion, these gentle blooms would be forced by unseasonal icy blasts to retreat back to the sod and its safety.

And I had my summer of rebirth. As my beautiful blossoms grew and reached toward the sunlight, so did my heart and my mind and soul reach toward the light of God.

In retracing all these seasons of my life, a fuller understanding of love has come to pass. I now realize love is not a fleeting feeling that leaves just because a relationship ends. It is not some whimsical mood related to romance. Love is a state of being that has remained laced inside my soul. It has come to me in many forms, depending upon the type of connection I've had to those I've loved, but I have kept every instance laced to my soul.

For me, love came in the form of my father, a man who taught me to love with conviction and loyalty. He showed me that despite our flaws and imperfections, what was important was to stand tall and respect those who form our family.

Love came in the form of a woman I called Mother. Ours was not an easy connection, but it helped me to evolve into the woman I am today. In mentoring me on the path to womanhood, she allowed me to find myself and to move to my own unique rhythm of life.

Love, too, has come in the form of my daughter and my grandchildren. For in this love, I've learned what it can be at its most pure. It helped me to fully comprehend the deep bonds that can exist between souls. In the quietest of moments of my motherhood, I found a peace and love that does not compare to any other I have ever felt or found.

My love for the men in my life has also come with seasons of its own. I now realize that love does not always end, but transcends intermittent memories of what was. This type stays deeply hidden inside the recesses of our hearts and minds and, on occasion, peeks out to remind us of the importance of opening our hearts to love again.

The love I've felt for my family members came with the sustained understanding that despite the conflicts between us, when the going gets tough, you can count on them to rally around and help. The love I have for my siblings reminds me that we humans are never alone, we merely have to reach out and ask for assistance.

With respect to the love of friends, I have become keenly aware that the pathways in our lives lead us to those who will help to make life easier. True friends remind us to laugh and to take notice of the little things. In their company, we can feel togetherness in times of joy and sorrow as well.

And I have learned all too well the meaning of love as it relates to God. I have found this love is the strongest of all. It is the very essence of life. It brings us to the universal energy that renews our lives each and every day. It is a connection that gives our souls permission to believe in a greater force as we forge ahead to grow and improve our lots in life. It is the framework for the process of birth, life, death, and rebirth into the everlasting universe and our ascension into its light.

What I have learned about this miracle called love is that contemplating it leads to the opening of the mind, and that traveling further down its path leads directly to a rapture of the heart and soul. It revitalizes the senses and merges with all our temporal knowledge to sustain our lives. It protects us and brings about the necessary changes that allow us to grow and reach out to others. Regardless of its form—daughter, sister, wife, mother, lover, or friend—it can produce the same result. Love is indeed the rhythm behind the dance of life that brings about revelatory experiences of joy, sadness, and redemption. Love unites the heart, mind, and soul into one; when this happens, we experience a state of euphoria. This heightened state of awareness then expands our abilities to move forward and thrive. It is the ultimate state of understanding and our link between our humanity and spirituality.

Here, in the closing passages of this book, I look to my angelic guides for their assistance once again. I pray for the ability to open my heart and to embrace love in a manner worthy of my caring spirit. I hope to redeem myself by recapturing the love I know dwells deep within. If indeed it is time to allow for new love to find a home inside my heart, I pray that the pathway to it may be illuminated by the light of God.

EPILOGUE

A Knowing Sensitive

As I've traveled around the country conducting book signings and workshops, sharing my life experiences, I have had the pleasure of meeting so many fascinating individuals, many of whom were open to their intuitive gifts. I've heard stories about the moment they felt, heard, or saw an angelic being. They usually convey their experiences in terms of childlike wonder at the beauty of the encounters and how their lives were forever altered by them. As I listen, my mind often recalls the teachings of my Catholic upbringing and I hear the words of the Apostle Matthew ring in my ears: "Again I say to you, if two of you agree on Earth about anything they ask, it will be done for them by my Father in Heaven. For where two or three are gathered in my name, there am I among them."

And so it was at each gathering. The presence of God shined through. His grace was evident in the faces of all who spoke to me, and was mirrored in the light of their eyes and the love in their hearts.

For many years, I toiled against and struggled with my gifts. At times, I even perceived them to be a curse instead of a blessing. As I grew to accept them, I learned to trust completely what I was feeling, hearing, or seeing. In awakening the power of my soul, I reconnected to my relationship with God. After periods of silence, I hear laughter and music once more. I have felt my heart expand and I am now better able to both give and receive love. With my heart and mind now wide open, I have come to accept that the knowledge I have acquired comes from God. I am blessed to be sensitive enough to feel the presence and hear the whisperings of the angels and to be able to see all that is meant to be seen.

In forging ahead toward the enlightenment of my spirit, I have found my place on this earthly domain. In the awakening of my soul, my spiritual purpose has merged with my human dreams and desires. It is my belief that the trials and tribulations of life have resulted in my learning great lessons. They were the preparation I needed for better things yet to be. This amazing journey has allowed me to release my bitterness and fears, to forgive myself and others, to refresh my heart, replenish my mind, and renew my spirit. I am now in a period of revitalization. In the time I have left on this earth, I welcome the chance to allow myself to be my authentic self.

Adonai Elohim . . .

ABOUT THE AUTHOR

Lillie Leonardi worked in law enforcement for more than 25 years before retiring to pursue her lifelong dream of writing. In 1984, Leonardi was appointed to serve as the first female police officer with the city of Arnold, Pennsylvania. She broke barriers again in 1994, when she was appointed the first female chief of police for Chatham College. In 1998, Leonardi joined the FBI (Pittsburgh Division) as the Community Outreach Specialist, where she served until 2010.

www.lillieleonardi.com

Hay House Titles of Related Interest

YOU CAN HEAL YOUR LIFE, the movie,
starring Louise Hay & Friends
(available as a 1-DVD programme and an expanded 2-DVD set)
Watch the trailer at: www.LouiseHayMovie.com

THE SHIFT, the movie,
starring Dr Wayne W. Dyer
(available as a 1-DVD programme and an expanded 2-DVD set)
Watch the trailer at: www.DyerMovie.com

ANGELS WHISPER IN MY EAR:
Incredible Stories of Hope and Love from the Angels, by Kyle Gray

MARY, QUEEN OF ANGELS, by Doreen Virtue

THE MIRACLES OF ARCHANGEL MICHAEL, by Doreen Virtue

All of the above are available at your local bookstore,
or may be ordered by contacting Hay House (see next page).

NOTES

NOTES

NOTES

NOTES

HAY HOUSE

Look within

Join the conversation about latest products,
events, exclusive offers and more.

f   Hay House UK

🐦   @HayHouseUK

📷   @hayhouseuk

❤   healyourlife.com

We'd love to hear from you!